ANNA KARENINA

Borgo Press Books Translated by FRANK J. MORLOCK

Anna Karenina: A Play in Five Acts, by Edmond Guiraud, from the Novel by Leo Tolstoy

Anthony: A Play in Five Acts, by Alexandre Dumas, Père

The Children of Captain Grant: A Play in Five Acts, by Jules Verne and Adolphe d'Ennery

Crime and Punishment: A Play in Three Acts, by Frank J. Morlock, from the Novel by Fyodor Dostoyevsky

Falstaff: A Play in Four Acts, by William Shakespeare, John Dennis, William Kendrick, and Frank J. Morlock

Jesus of Nazareth: A Play in Three Acts, by Paul Demasy

Joan of Arc: A Play in Five Acts, by Charles Desnoyer

The Lily in the Valley: A Play in Five Acts, by Théodore Barrière and Arthur de Beauplan, from the Novel by Honoré de Balzac

Michael Strogoff: A Play in Five Acts, by Adolphe d'Ennery and Jules Verne

The Mysteries of Paris: A Play in Five Acts, by Eugène Sue and Prosper Dinaux

Peau de Chagrin: A Play in Five Acts, by Louis Judicis, from the Novel by Honoré de Balzac

A Raw Youth: A Play in Five Acts, by Frank J. Morlock, from the Novel by Fyodor Dostoyevsky

Richard Darlington: A Play in Three Acts, by Alexandre Dumas, Père

The San Felice: A Play in Five Acts, by Maurice Drack, from the Novel by Alexander Dumas, Père

Shylock, the Merchant of Venice: A Play in Three Acts, by Alfred de Vigny

The Voyage Through the Impossible: A Play in Three Acts, by Adolphe d'Ennery and Jules Verne

William Shakespeare: A Play in Six Acts, by Ferdinand Dugué

ANNA KARENINA

A PLAY IN FIVE ACTS

by

EDMOND GUIRAUD
FROM THE NOVEL BY LEO TOLSTOY

Translated and Adapted by Frank J. Morlock

THE BORGO PRESS

An Imprint of Wildside Press LLC

MMIX

Copyright © 2009 by Frank J. Morlock

All rights reserved. No part of this book may be reproduced without the expressed written consent of the author. Professionals are warned that this material, being fully protected under the copyright laws of the United States of America, and all other countries of the Berne and Universal Copyright Convention, is subject to a royalty. All rights, including all forms of performance now existing or later invented, but not limited to professional, amateur, recording, motion picture, recitation, public reading, radio, television broadcasting, DVD, and Role Playing Games, and all rights of translation into foreign languages, are expressly reserved. Particular emphasis is placed on the question of readings, and all uses of these plays by educational institutions, permission for which must be secured in advance from the author's publisher, Wildside Press, 9710 Traville Gateway Dr. #234, Rockville, MD 20850 (phone 301-762-1305). Printed in the United States of America

www.wildsidepress.com

FIRST WILDSIDE EDITION

CONTENTS

Cast of Characters 7

Act I 9
Act II, Scene 1 43
Act II, Scene 2 73
Act III 87
Act IV 114
Act V 133
Epilogue 153

Marlborough's Song from Act I, Scene 1 159

About the Author 162

DEDICATION

To

***GERRY TETRAULT**, my lifelong friend*

CAST OF CHARACTERS

Prince Stefan Arkadyevich Oblonsky (Stiva)
Princess Darya Alexandrovna (Dolly), his wife
Grisha, Tania, and Vasya, his children
Mlle Roland, governess in Oblonsky household
Matvei, Oblonsky's valet
Anna Arkadyevna Karenina, Oblonsky's sister
Constantin Dimitrievich Levin
Alexei Alexandrovich Karenin, Anna's husband
Princess Kitty Shcherbatskaia, Dolly's sister
Prince Shcherbatsky, Dolly and Kitty's father
Princess Shcherbatskaia, Dolly and Kitty's mother
Count Alexei Kirillovich Vronsky
Seriozha Alexeivitch, Anna's son
Princess Miaghkaia
Countess Nordstone
Lieutenant Yavshine
Lieutenant Makhotin
Princess Somatoff
Prince Somatoff
Princess Betsy Tverskaia
Monsieur Cord, horse trainer
Sergei Ivanovich Koznishev, Levin's brother
Countess Lidia Ivanovna
Vassilii Lukich, Seriozha's tutor
General Golenishchev
Vladimir
Anita Campanetti

General Serpukhovskoy
Kapitonich
Matrona Niania
Popoff
Annoushka
Peter
Nicolas
Princess Barbe

ACT I

First Tableau

In Moscow. The study of Stefan Arkadyevich Oblonsky (Stiva). To the left, a great arch opens on the reception hall. At the rise of the curtain, the children dance a roundelay with their French governess.

Mlle Roland: Do the chorus again, all three of you and don't shout so loud, Grisha. And you, Vasya, why do you want to cry? Come on, sing like little French children.

Grisha: Me, I am a colonel in the Russian Army. Colonel of the Guards, not French!

Mlle Roland: But, of course, Grisha, you are a colonel. But a colonel must know how to sing, to give an example to his soldiers. Come on.

(Mlle Roland holds hands with the children as they sing a song in French about Marlboro.) [The complete lyrics are given at the end of the play.]

Grisha: This Marlboro's an Englishman, right?

Mlle Roland: Yes, Grisha. Come on! Sing.

(All sing again. Stiva enters and joins hands with them.)

Stiva: La Trinité se passe.

Grisha: Papa, Papa!

Stiva: Hush. Let's finish the song.

All: La Trinité se passem
 Malbrough ne revient pas.

Stiva: Bravo, Mademoiselle.

Vasya: You know the song, too, Papa?

(The children applaud and embrace Stiva.)

Grisha: But, of course, Vasya! A Prince knows everything. Papa is a Prince. Everybody else knows nothing, but he knows everything.

Mlle Roland: Grisha is very proud.

Stiva: (laughing) Bah! It's a Russian characteristic, Mlle Roland. It's necessary for every race to have its national fault. Are you sure that you don't have three or four?

Mlle Roland: I don't know, sir.

Stiva: Hum! You don't know! I could perhaps mention some of your pretty national faults.

Mlle Roland: Ah!

Stiva: Yes! Hum!

(During this short exchange the children have approached their father's bureau.)

Stiva: (to the children) Grisha, stay out of my bureau. (to Mlle Roland) Why do the children always want to play there, Mademoiselle?

Mlle Roland: The playroom has been done over for the reception and Madame advised me to use your study. "Go there," she said, "it's a study where my husband never works."

Stiva: Oh, very nice! You mock me.

Mlle Roland: Pardon me, sir.

Stiva: Of course, of course. It's charming. (to the children) Grisha, Tania, Vasya, come over here. Wait—go to the dining room. Yes, the buffet is ready and no one's here yet. Mlle Roland will follow shortly.

(All the children go out by the center door. Stiva prevents Mlle Roland from following the children.)

Stiva: Stay here.

Mlle Roland: But, I assure you—

Stiva: (pressing her hand and laughing) Come on—the right of passage. You know very well that you madden me with your charm. It's inebriating. Ah, pretty French girl. Come on, a little kiss. Let's see.

Mlle Roland: (protecting herself rather poorly) Leave me—the children—the Princess. Look here, sir. (she laughs) This is governess abuse.

(Stiva takes Mlle Roland in his arms and embraces her, despite her resistance. At this moment Dolly enters and screams in indignant stupefaction.)

Dolly: Oh! Oh! (to Mlle Roland) Get out! Get out!

Mlle Roland: I assure you, Madame—

(Mlle Roland begins to exit by the center door.)

Dolly: Not that way. Not to the children. You must never see them again. It would soil them. The mistress of their father. Oh, fie, how ugly it is.

(Dolly begins to cry, suddenly, heavy tears. Stiva makes a sign to Mlle Roland to leave. He is very annoyed, and after the governess leaves, he tries smiling naively and explaining to his wife.)

Stiva: Listen, Dolly. Listen to me.

Dolly: No—you are base—without a heart—without morality. I intend to leave you immediately, to never see you. Oh—no—never to see you.

Stiva: A minute of straying!

Dolly: I put you on a pedestal like a god. I gave you three beautiful children. I, the most scrupulous of women. Is it possible that you can be so vile? The lowest—the lowest of men.

Stiva: (smiling) I assure you, without being the lowest of men, one can—

Dolly: (stupefied by his smile, more indignant, more violent) You can laugh. You have the strength to laugh. Oh, coward, coward, villain. Leave me. Don't touch me. Leave me.

(Dolly exits quickly and leaves Stiva disconcerted. Stiva goes to a mirror and looks at himself.)

Stiva: (after a short pause) It's true. I smiled. It's the smile of an animal who has lost everything. She'd commenced to weaken—and all was going so well. Bah! Everything will sort itself out. (still in front of the mirror, looking at himself complacently) No one would believe I'm my wife's age. (calling) Matvei, Matvei! Where are you, imbecile? (suddenly, in a bad temper) Everything is going wrong today!

(Enter Matvei, an old family servant. He is fifty years old and wearing livery.)

Matvei: Your Excellency rang?

Stiva: Where have you been?

Matvei: With Vasily, Excellency, setting up the green plants in the hall. We hardly have time before the guests arrive.

Stiva: (very upset) The guests! Ah, devil! I have completely forgotten them. Everything must be arranged—at least in a provisional way.

Matvei: We are doing our very best, Excellency.

Stiva: Yes, yes. That's not what I meant to say. Anna Arkadyevna—is she at home?

Matvei: What does your Excellency wish to say?

Stiva: I'm asking you if my sister, Madame Karenina is home. Go find her. Tell her I must speak to her immediately.

(Stiva pushes Matvei toward the door.)

Matvei: (returning) I forgot to tell you, Excellency, Constantin Dimitrievich Levin is here to see you.

Stiva: Levin, Levin. It's just the right moment. Go quickly as I told you and bring back her reply!

(Matvei leaves. Stiva goes to the center door.)

Stiva: Levin! Levin!

(Levin enters. He is in a peasant outfit and boots. He has a timid, modest demeanor.)

Levin: Good day, Stiva.

Stiva: Hello, old roughneck. (pointing to his costume) Eh! Eh! Always faithful to tradition, huh? A true peasant. I can give you a minute. Tell me, what brings you to Moscow?

Levin: I'm glad you're so pressed. I will tell you simply—it's this way—

Stiva: (laughing very hard) Really, truly? You wouldn't prefer a nice fashionable jacket and a flower in your buttonhole? No? That's always secondary. (passing from one subject to another in a disconcerting hurry) Do you know that my marriage is ruined? I stupidly let myself be surprised by my wife while I was tickling Mlle Roland's chin.

Levin: Oh, Stiva—the governess of the little ones?

Stiva: Then, you know, Dolly —cries, tears, nerves. At four o'clock in the afternoon, a tragic breakup. "I am going to my mother." For a silly kiss—nothing at all. Ah, if my sister Anna doesn't step in at this moment, I can only hope for a miracle to save me.

Levin: Anna Arkadyevna is a woman of great sense.

Stiva: My sister is of an unbounded intelligence and of a rare virtue. (laughing) It's a family trait! And, to tell you, that at five o'clock we have a reception— It's absolutely necessary for society, for me, to get back with my wife—at least between five and seven.

Levin: I came intentionally a little in advance.

Stiva: True. You'll be one of us one day, naturally. Well, tell me later the reason you've abandoned the handle of your plough. Would you like a cigar?

Levin: (trying to regroup before this wave of words) No, no. You know it's a question of— My most dearest wish is to become your brother-in-law. It's some months since I've first adored Kitty Shcherbatskaia—without daring to tell her. So—should I throw myself before her today? I still haven't said anything to Kitty. But perhaps, your wife—her sister—or you, even your mother-in-law,—because I am not sure of the sympathy of the Prince. Anyway, you understand me.

Stiva: (laughing) Yes, though you're still not very clear.

But, go on—you please me. You are a perfect man. We understand each other so well and you will help me on your part in the future, vis-à-vis, my wife.

Levin: Then, on your advice, I ought to declare myself?

Stiva: You ought to! One always ought to. First, because one risks nothing, and if it happens, one can have no regrets.

Levin: That's not the way I look at the thing.

Stiva: (pulling him) My God, you are amorous. Really, you can't stay here a minute longer, go into my little smoking room. I will come back to you. I am not going to upset myself over you. Well— (Anna enters) Ah, Anna.

Anna: Well, Mr. Levin. Do I make you flee? Good day.

Stiva: (pushing Levin towards the door of the little smoking room) You can say hello later.

Levin: (laughing) What can one say to that? He's pushing me out the door.

Anna: Excuse him.

Levin: But I don't mind.

(Levin leaves.)

Anna: You were not very polite to your friend.

Stiva: Right now I haven't the time. Something is happening, right now.

Anna: Yes, I am informed.

Stiva: What?

Anna: Your wife saw you kissing Mlle Roland and intends to leave you. She judges your action very severely. She's right. What you have done is shameful. I can't find words to defend you. And if I pardon you in the depths of my heart, it's because you're only an overgrown child, stupid but not evil, despite all. Still I can only deplore such a lack of moral sense.

Stiva: Yes. But this is not the time to speak of moral sensibility. It's necessary to conceal things immediately. The reception is nearly upon us. She's giving it in honor of your stay here in Moscow. Dolly must be here to receive our guests. What will your husband think? What will the world think if she doesn't appear?

Anna: (ironically) It's always the world's opinion that preoccupies you.

Stiva: Should it not to be first in the mind of high state bureaucrats?

Anna: Well, what do you want me to do?

Stiva: Go find Dolly and convince her to safeguard appearances. Tell her it's her duty—that she ought to make this sacrifice. After all, she's never been unhappy—and it's only a question of a kiss. That's all. Just a kiss.

Anna: How can you be so gay, Stiva?

Stiva: (flippant) Gay! Gay! I am not gay. But I've got a nature different from yours, more adventurous. You—you're as virtuous as you are pretty. And you are certainly to be praised for remaining faithful to your husband, minister of State, Alexei Alexandrovich Karenin, who is really the most cold—

Anna: Stiva!

Stiva: Right! Absolutely right! Go speak to Dolly. You have a pretty dress. Oh, an idea! If Dolly—one must foresee things—if Dolly won't hear reason, you will do the honors. We will pretend my wife is ill.

Anna: We will see. Wait for me here. It won't be a happy solution.

Stiva: Hurry! Here's a carriage already arriving. (at the window) My father-in-law—the family, Kitty.

(Anna leaves in haste. Stiva accompanies her to the door.)

Stiva:(calling)
Matvei! Matvei! You'll bring Prince and Princess Shcherbatsky in here. (alone) All this is very troublesome. (at the mirror) Still, my appearance is excellent.

(Enter Princess and Prince Shcherbatsky and Kitty.)

Princess Shcherbatskaia: We've come a bit ahead of time. Kitty's got it into her head to be helpful to Dolly and Anna so they can receive the guests.

Stiva: Eh! It's a good idea. Good day, mother, my dear father-in-law. Good day, little sister.

Prince Shcherbatsky: Plague take the pigheadedness of

women to drag me to this type of reception.

Princess Shcherbatskaia: Where are Dolly and Anna?

Stiva: Not quite ready yet, naturally.

Princess Shcherbatskaia: We could go to them, Kitty and I.

Stiva: Not at all—not at all. They know you're here. I saw you get out of your carriage and mentioned it to Anna.

Princess Shcherbatskaia: (to Prince Shcherbatsky) But, my dear, you look very angry.

Prince Shcherbatsky: In fact, I am. You have neither pride nor dignity.

Stiva: (to Kitty) Fire burning.

Kitty: What?

Stiva: Things are not right between your father and mother. There's an ill wind blowing in both households.

Kitty: Oh, Stiva.

Stiva: (low to Kitty) Come on. Let's leave them alone. Come with me. It's better for them to fight before the guests arrive. (aloud) We are going to see if everything is ready.

(Stiva and Kitty leave.)

Prince Shcherbatsky: Fine! Neither pride nor dignity. You are losing your daughter with this base and ridiculous way of finding her a husband.

Princess Shcherbatskaia: But, in heaven's name, Prince! What have I done?

Prince Shcherbatsky: What have you done? First you have attracted a suitor about whom all Moscow is talking about. And what is worse, a type of parade-ground officer, this Vronsky, that I don't like by half.

Princess Shcherbatskaia: Count Alexei Vronsky is a man absolutely worthy of esteem.

Prince Shcherbatsky: His mother wielded a broom during my day at Court.

Princess Shcherbatskaia: Her son cannot be responsible. He's an accomplished officer who has a brilliant future, thanks to his own merit and his relatives at Court. He's a superb catch for our daughter.

Prince Shcherbatsky: Agreed!

Princess Shcherbatskaia: Besides, the children love each other.

Prince Shcherbatsky: (clapping) Oh, I was waiting for the great argument! That our Kitty has the image of him in her head and heart, I don't question at all. But, who can promise me that he reciprocates?

Princess Shcherbatskaia: You will be reassured soon. Count Vronsky is already morally engaged to Kitty and ought to declare himself this very day.

Prince Shcherbatsky: Praise God! But I would have preferred Levin. Now there's an honest man.

Princess Shcherbatskaia: Without doubt, an honest man. But, also a type of gentleman-farmer who dresses like a Russian and smells like a peasant. Can you see this peasant as the husband of our exquisite, worldly Kitty?

Prince Shcherbatsky: I would prefer a peasant for a son-in-law than another Stiva. Good—everything's fine. I'll shut up.

Princess Shcherbatskaia: Dolly is very happy.

Prince Shcherbatsky: She isn't hard to please.

(This discussion is interrupted by the entry of Anna.)

Princess Shcherbatskaia: Good day, Anna Arkadyevna.

Anna: Good day, Princess. Good day, Prince.

Prince Shcherbatsky: Madame.

Anna: Kitty is here, too?

Princess Shcherbatskaia: Certainly, with Stiva and the children.

Prince Shcherbatsky: Have you good news of the Court, Madame Karenina?

Anna: Excellent, thanks.

Princess Shcherbatskaia: And your dear little Seriozha?

Anna: He writes me every day.

Prince Shcherbatsky: At twelve years old! It's remarkable.

Anna: He's very intelligent and he loves me. How have I been able to remain here so long without embracing him? My little dear. Now, soon, I can get ready.

Princess Shcherbatskaia: Your stay in Moscow draws to a close?

Anna: Eh, yes! Just think, I've been here more than fifteen days already. I've never been separated from my little Seriozha that long.

Princess Shcherbatskaia: Is Dolly ready?

Anna: Almost. She only asked me to hurry her husband. (smiling) She wanted him to have the satisfaction of being the first to see her new toilette.

(Anna begins to move toward the door to the grand salon.)

Princess Shcherbatskaia: (to Prince Shcherbatsky) Well—you see—your ridiculous pessimism! They are more amorous than in their first days.

Prince Shcherbatsky: Hum! So much the better!

Anna: (in the distance) Do you permit me to call Stiva?

Princess Shcherbatskaia: But, yes! And Kitty, and the children. I want to embrace all of them.

Anna: Stiva! Stiva! Kitty! Children! They love you, oh, yes, they love you. They're pillaging the buffet. Well, when Mamma finds out.

(Enter Kitty, Stiva, and the children.)

Grisha: It's Papa and Kitty. We started—

Stiva: Oh, the little liar, fie!

Prince Shcherbatsky: Come, my little angels. Come hug grandfather and grandmamma.

Grisha: Yes. You, grandfather, but grandmother pinches.

Princess Shcherbatskaia: What do you mean I pinch?

Grisha: Yes, your chin pinches.

Anna: Grisha!

Prince Shcherbatsky: Ah! Ah! Ah! The little bugger—he's right.

Princess Shcherbatskaia: That's an absurd joke. Besides, these children ought to be in their room with their governess.

Anna: (low to Stiva) Go, Stiva! Go to Dolly! She's expecting you. And try to obtain her pardon.

Stiva: (low) You have been able to obtain that! Ah, Anna, you are—you are a great man.

Anna: (low) And you—a great fool! Come now, go quickly. (aloud) You are excused. I've already explained to the Princess that your wife wants to show you her new toilette first.

Stiva: Then, I am going quickly. (low to Anna) Thanks,

the reception will be cordial, intimate. There's such a joy in living after wiping out an argument.

Princess Shcherbatskaia: Stiva, are you taking the children to Mlle Roland?

Stiva: Huh? Yes— No— Oh! No, impossible! Well, for goodness sake—you have unusual ideas.

(Stiva leaves.)

Princess Shcherbatskaia: Why so unusual?

Anna: Because Mlle Roland is no longer here, as of today. She was abruptly recalled to France—because of the sudden illness of a close relative.

Princess Shcherbatskaia: Oh, that's a bizarre thing. And who's going to take care of the children now?

Anna: Dolly and I—until a new regime is established.

Kitty: And I! Oh, yes, Mamma. I love them so much.

Grisha: Me, too. I love you.

Anna: What pretensions, Kitty.

Princess Shcherbatskaia: Fine, you take care of them, that's agreed—until you've found a new governess. For the moment, they must be sent to their chamber with their nurse.

Prince Shcherbatsky: Or with me! It would amuse me more than to listen to the chatter of you silly women over the tea cups.

Grisha: Yes, yes! Grandpapa, come with us. We will play at hunting.

Prince Shcherbatsky: That's a good idea.

Grisha: Hunting a bear.

Tania: You will be the bear!

Prince Shcherbatsky: Naturally!

Anna: What a love, this little Tania.

Princess Shcherbatskaia: Get going, all four of you. The biggest child, it's always you, Prince.

Prince Shcherbatsky: Eh! Eh! You're so youthful in character and tastes. It's necessary to put me in tune.

Anna: I am taking Kitty for our last preparations, if it doesn't bore her to stay alone with her old friend.

Princess Shcherbatskaia: Nothing will be more agreeable to her, Anna! If you knew how fond she is of you. Well, come little ones. Go on ahead.

(Prince Shcherbatsky, Princess Shcherbatskaia, Grisha, Tanya, and Vasya leave, center back.)

Anna: Is it true, Kitty, that you love me to this extremity?

Kitty: It is true. And I admire you, too, because you are what I want to become—a real woman.

Anna: You have real taste, Kitty. You are beautiful.

Kitty: Less beautiful than you!

Anna: No, no. It's not necessary to make me blush from an excess of compliments.

Kitty: That's not a compliment!

Anna: Ah, young girls—what a happy outlook they have on life—when their hearts are pleased. How seductive everything appears to the eyes of one in love!

Kitty: Oh—that makes me blush.

Anna: Come on, don't dissimulate. I am up to date. Stiva has told me. I met Vronsky several times in society; he pleases me a lot. I know he has a very beautiful nature, loyal and chivalrous. I'd be enchanted if it came about.

Kitty: Me, I admit to you that I saw nothing for a long while—and I know that today will be decisive. Mama has told me that he will make a declaration—without a doubt.

Anna: That's why you are happier than ever. You have the beauty of joy to come.

Kitty: And you, the beauty of joy that is.

Anna: Ah, I give such an impression?

Kitty: Without a doubt! Are you unaware of it?

Anna: No, no.

(Matvei opens both wings of the door to the grand salon. One can see Stiva and Dolly talking amicably. One can hear the voice of Stiva.)

Stiva: Then your father absolutely insisted on playing the bear with Tania and your mother took Grisha's joke very badly.

Dolly: What did he say to her then?

Stiva: That she pricked him on the chin when she embraced him. Ah! Ah!

Dolly: How crazy you are, Stiva, to repeat that.

Stiva: Crazy? No, I find this remark so judicious.

(Stiva and Dolly come into the main acting area.)

Stiva: (low to Anna) All is saved!

Anna: (low to Stiva) Except for honor!

Stiva: The reception will be pleasant and cordial. That was the essential point.

Dolly: (going to Kitty and embracing her effusively) Hello, my little sister.

Kitty: Hello, my dear Dolly. How beautiful you are! And how your eyes shine.

Dolly: How do you like my gown, Kitty? Oh, but yours is delicious. There's simply no question of resisting such a pretty temptress.

Matvei: (announcing in the grand salon) The Princess Miaghkaia.

Princess Miaghkaia: (entering, a little pretentious) What a pleasure. I am so happy to be the first to arrive. (to Kitty with a confidential tone) You are exquisite. I believe that I met him in society, my dear. I am sure he's absolutely mad about you.

Stiva: (approaching) Saints above! Princess, you have the most admirably sensitive eyes that I know.

Princess Miaghkaia: (to Dolly) You have a perfect husband—and so gallant.

Anna: Yes! Stiva is one of the perpetual gallants.

Dolly: Perhaps it would be more correct to go to the grand salon to await the arrival of our guests?

Princess Miaghkaia: Ah, my God. We are very numerous. I am such a great savage.

Stiva: It is true, with such pensive eyes.

Anna: (irritated) Stiva, do you know exactly who is coming today?

Stiva: Yes, yes. Well, naturally Vronsky, Lieutenant Makhotin—

Matvei: (announcing) The Countess Nordstone.

Countess Nordstone: (entering) Long live the army!

Stiva: Here's a triumphal arrival.

Dolly: Stiva, we numbered the invitations today.

Countess Nordstone: And he forgot me?

Stiva: How can one forget you, once one has seen you?

Countess Nordstone: Thank you. With me, they don't succeed.

Stiva: What?

Countess Nordstone: The insipid ones.

Princess Miaghkaia: That's right. You won't put up with them.

Countess Nordstone: Hello, delicious Kitty. What a fresh outfit. A real rose bud.

Matvei: (announcing) The Lieutenants Yavshine and Makhotin.

Countess Nordstone: He hasn't come yet. Are you coming, pretty Kitty?

(In the grand salon, a group is forming for a reception. The Princess Shcherbatskaia, Dolly, Anna, Stiva, Countess Nordstone, the Lieutenants, the new arrivals all leave. Kitty with Princess Miaghkaia who brings Kitty toward the rest.)

Princess Miaghkaia: Shall we stay here a bit? I have to speak with my little Kitty about something dear to her.

(At that instant, Stiva reenters, laughing)

Stiva: Am I stupid! Am I stupid? I left him, completely forgotten, in the smoking room.

Princess Miaghkaia: Who, Stiva?

Stiva: Eh, my friend Levin. Constantin Levin, who has been there all alone for an hour.

Princess Miaghkaia: Constantin Levin! My intimate enemy! The lover of my pretty Kitty!

Stiva: Himself, Princess. And I am going to put him between your claws in delivering him.

Kitty: God, how unhappy I am going to be.

Princess Miaghkaia: Why, my dear?

Kitty: He prowled around me with such supplications. And then, today—exactly—he treated me in such a way as seemed to me particularly guilty.

Princess Miaghkaia: (suddenly very coquettish) Oh. Stiva?

Stiva: Princess?

Princess Miaghkaia: How is she behaving now?

Kitty: Languorously and maddening.

Princess Miaghkaia: Hum! Kitty, don't listen! (to Stiva) Suppose you decided to do a little thing to earn some gratitude in her eyes?

Stiva: Tell me what I must do. I will do anything—a miracle!

Princess Miaghkaia: Good! Go back to the grand salon.

Stiva: Huh? But, Levin, I am going before—

Princess Miaghkaia: No, no, go back to the grand salon and continue to forget Levin. He's ruining our plans today.

Stiva: But, why?

Matvei: (announcing) The Count Alexei Kirillovich Vronsky.

Kitty: (radiant) Ah!

Princess Miaghkaia: (pointing to Kitty) Wait! Hear my response.

Stiva: The devil! Levin is my friend and—

Princess Miaghkaia: And here—the reward as promised, with a tip.

(Princess Miaghkaia gives Stiva her hand to kiss.)

Stiva: (sadly, looking at the smoking room door) Let's get going! Just now, Constantin Levin, I sold you out.

Princess Miaghkaia: For more than thirty pieces of silver.

Stiva: For a smile. (laughing) At least there's a good wine cellar there, a divan and some excellent cigars. Should I go find my friend Vronsky?

Princess Miaghkaia: They call that going over to the enemy, bag and baggage.

Stiva: I don't do anything by half.

(Stiva leaves.)

Kitty: How good Stiva is.

Princess Miaghkaia: Yes, my Kitty, you find him good because he serves your projects, but he serves them to your detriment with his perfect dignity. Still, I don't wish to moralize—we profit too much from his attitudes— You aren't listening to me.

Kitty: Am I really very well dressed?

Princess Miaghkaia: Adorably.

(Enter Stiva with Vronsky.)

Stiva: I bring you a handsome officer. Vronsky, you know the Princess—and you know Kitty. To the devil with ceremony. Here, we are in the corner of no ceremony.

Princess Miaghkaia: Aren't they going to find our isolation extraordinary?

Stiva: Absolutely in order. We are here with the tacit agreement of everyone. We two chaperons, and these two—these two to look in each others' eyes. Come here, Princess.

Princess Miaghkaia: Yes, but take care! You've already had a glove from me and a kiss on my hand. I'm not disposed to give you anything else.

(Little by little the other guests arrive in the grand salon which has the joyous animation of an elegant and frivolous reception. The isolation of the office is almost absolute because of this.)

Vronsky: (to Kitty) Do you know that I have almost persuaded the Princess to take you to Tsarkoe Selo for the races in the next two weeks?

Kitty: Oh! How happy I am! I will see your pretty Froufrou whom you abandoned at St. Petersburg with such regret! That little filly holds a great place in your thoughts, Alexei Kirillovich.

Vronsky: No—not in my thoughts, rather in my favorite occupations. My thoughts are occupied by more noble images—more beautiful.

Kitty: Ah! Without a doubt, your ambitions as a soldier.

Vronsky: Why not try to speak a little less of my thoughts than of my heart?

Kitty: Because a young girl is very ignorant of these things. Hush! And when are you returning to St. Petersburg?

Vronsky: In three or four days.

Kitty: At the same time as Anna Arkadyevna! And, you will return?

Vronsky: But it depends on a single person—if my return will be very soon.

Stiva: (to Princess Miaghkaia) I believe we are completely unnoticed.

Princess Miaghkaia: That's the moment to reappear in the eyes of the world.

Stiva: But, on the contrary! Ah, wait, Countess Nordstone is at the piano. What is that scatterbrain going to play for us? Some little French ditties?

(Prelude in the corridor.)

Princess Miaghkaia: Yes, by Beethoven, "Sonata du Claire de Lune." She plays it much differently—with great feeling. She is a little hysterical.

Vronsky: (to Kitty) You haven't answered my question.

Kitty: Because my reply would be—so serious that—I prefer—not to give one at all and then, I thought that a young girl—

(Anna comes in unexpectedly.)

Anna: Pardon me for interrupting your conversations. I am very impressed by that music.

Stiva: I thought you were better balanced, Anna?

Anna: Nice. For you then, equilibrium resides in passivity and indifference?

Vronsky: Stiva has disconcerting opinions.

Anna: Isn't that true, sir?

Vronsky: One can be perfectly normal and sane, yet vibrate strangely to the depths of one's being before a perfect work of art or a prodigious spectacle of nature, or a play, or in hearing Beethoven—as at present! I don't believe I'm a degenerate, my dear Stiva, and my profession ought to make me control my emotions. Yet, it often happens to me that I am the slave of my impressions.

Stiva: Comic officer!

Princess Miaghkaia: Shut up, then, you materialist.

Anna: Then, truly, I am not very troublesome? I admit that I was a little tired out by the manners of your friend Lieutenant Makhotin.

Stiva: Oh—him. He's a true soldier, eyes at ten paces, speaks at a gallop, and argues with a bayonet.

Princess Miaghkaia: What a Cossack!

Stiva: Do you say so! Just what you need, Cossacks. Don't mistake!

Princess Miaghkaia: You talk to me like one of your friends, the French singer at the Alhambra. You are much too—Russian!

Stiva: That's it—deny your country now!

Anna: (to Kitty and Vronsky) Yes, I understand that very wall. Everyone, in his life, has a mysterious corner—a sort of forewarning that— It won't bore you if I tell you I was struck by something when I first came to Moscow two weeks ago? I left St. Petersburg, quite sad about leaving my son, my little Seriozha—a mother exaggerates so many things. And also, I left my husband with the conviction that here, in Moscow, something would happen that would upset me profoundly. I had the great joy of traveling with your mother, the Countess Vronsky—who is an adorable woman. We spoke of our children—of you and my little Seriozha, right into the night. It goes without saying that you each have the quality of your age. I went to sleep a little reassured and I had a strange vision in my sleep. I was alone, in the night, in a white robe—near a railway line. It was very cold. I don't know why I felt, in my heart, an inexpressible anguish. Then, on the railway line, I saw a sort of old Mouzhik with a thick beard, with dead eyes—who, carrying a large sack on his back, stopped from time to time to dig into his sack, and while looking, he spoke hastily, in French, rolling his R's: "It's necessary to beat the sword, to pound it, to mould it," he said—and he was so hideous, so repugnant to look at. A train whistled in the distance. I saw it coming towards us, the growling locomotive. The little old man paid no attention and continued on his way with singular carelessness. The train came closer and seemed larger. I saw the big eyes of the machine rush towards us. Then, fifty, thirty, ten, the Mouzhik wouldn't swerve. I awoke screaming. Had the little Mouzhik been hit and flattened? I was only able to get to sleep just as we got to Moscow. Then I found you, Stiva, with Count Vronsky who came to meet his mother.

Stiva: Which ought to reassure you! Two men of our stamp put bad dreams to flight.

Anna: Yes, I was reassured. But, the explanation of my dream came even before we left the station.

Vronsky: Truly. One of the railway workers fell on the tracks right before our eyes. The train crushed the head of the poor wretch.

Stiva: Resembling the little Mouzhik of your dreams.

Anna: No! He was young, very young!

Stiva: Then, the little Mouzhik still lives. Long live the little Mouzhik.

Princess Miaghkaia: Is it possible to find a spirit less respectable than that of your brother, Anna Arkadyevna? With him one cannot raise a subject of art or psychology without exposing it to sarcasm.

Anna: I am not the guardian of my brother, dear Princess.

Princess Miaghkaia: What a shame for the world. Your influence would be so profitable to him.

Stiva: (to Princess Miaghkaia) You, you must have a weakness for my humble self. You attack me too often not to be falling in love with me.

Princess Miaghkaia: Stupid! Insupportable and ugly.

Vronsky: (to Anna) I will return soon to St. Petersburg, Madame. Dare I put myself at your service for this long trip? You came to Moscow with my mother. If the company of the baby you were discussing is not too boring, I would be happy to—

Anna: Thanks. No, thanks Alexei Kirillovich. The day for my departure isn't yet settled. It would be an indiscretion.

Kitty: And, if I insisted, my good friend? Let him be your *cavalier servante*. (low) You could look into so many things on which my happiness depends. You could speak of me.

Anna: I am not yet old enough, little Kitty, not to be compromised.

Kitty: Oh—your behavior is so perfect.

Vronsky: I could protect you, perhaps, from the little Mouzhik—if Mademoiselle Shcherbatskaia desires it.

Anna: I will see, I will see. If my little Kitty were to be jealous—

Kitty: (low to Anna) No. Listen to me, I am so happy. I wouldn't spoil the trip with remorse.

Anna: What have you to reproach yourself for, little girl?

Kitty: You know Constantin Dimitrievich Levin?

Anna: Yes. Didn't he come today?

Kitty: He did. He seemed—a little in love with me.

Anna: I know. But, it is too late, isn't it? The prize is taken.

Kitty: And—just now—I did something bad.

Anna: As bad as that?

Kitty: Stiva made him wait in his little smoking room.

Anna: I know. That's when I came.

Kitty: And, on my advice, at my request, Stiva forgot to go get him.

Anna: What are you telling me?

Kitty: So I could be alone with Vronsky—with my fiancé.

Anna: Why, you're very villainous.

Kitty: I know, but I don't love him.

Anna: And, is he still there? Stiva, is it possible that you've made a fool of your friend Levin?

Stiva: Huh? A farce! A joke.

Anna: Cruel. You have no heart.

Stiva: I did it without malice. To please the Princess.

Anna: Oh, it's an idea of hers. Never mind. We must make amends immediately. Now, Kitty, and you, Stiva, go away. I will take it on myself to make the excuse. I will say you left and I forgot.

Stiva: (to Princess Miaghkaia) The moment of punishment has come and the victim runs away.

Princess Miaghkaia: Leave, if you wish. I have the interests of my dear Kitty to protect. You are the only one—and you alone have betrayed—

Stiva: Oh, very nice. I should have expected that.

(Levin enters.)

Anna: How many excuses we owe you, Constantin Dimitrievich. My brother is so inept. I just realized your absence. You know everybody here.

Vronsky: I haven't the honor.

Anna: Then permit me to introduce you to each other. Monsieur Constantin Dimitrievich Levin. The Count Alexei Kirillovich Vronsky.

Vronsky: Enchanted, Monsieur.

Levin: Very happy, sir.

Princess Miaghkaia: (low to Levin) Engaged officially—Kitty from today, I tell you this, so you will be au courant.

Levin: I understand why they forgot me in the little smoking room.

(In the grand salon, there is applause for Countess Nordstone, who has finished playing.)

Kitty: (to Anna) You will permit Alexei Vronsky to protect you against the old Mouzhik?

Anna: Yes.

Kitty: How happy I am. Thank you, my good friend. I know that you will be a sort of beneficent genius.

Vronsky: A charmer! Anna Arkadyevna must have a slightly Bohemian soul.

(Stiva enters unexpectedly with Yavshine, Makhotin, and the Countess Nordstone.)

Stiva: Hoopla! The young folks—a great news. Will you permit them to waltz? Everything fine here?

Levin: I don't have the heart to dance, Stiva.

Stiva: Why, Constantin Dimitrievich? Oh, the devil. To the contrary! Distract yourself. Distract yourself! Pardon! Makhotin! Makhotin!

Makhotin: Huh?

Stiva: Have a dance. Invite your Princess?

Princess Miaghkaia: You are mad! If someone heard you!

Makhotin: Bah! Everybody is au courant.

Princess Miaghkaia: How do they know?

Makhotin: I told them!

Princess Miaghkaia: Brute!

Makhotin: I was.

Princess Miaghkaia: Go away. They're looking at us, go away.

(Prelude to a waltz in the corridor.)

Makhotin: Come on, come on, my little Columbine. Not so many moods!

Levin: (to Kitty) Would you give me this last waltz? The waltz of parting?

Kitty: Well, I don't know. (looking at Vronsky and Anna, who are speaking low and smiling) They're talking about me. (aloud) Yes.

(Kitty takes Levin's arm and the waltz begins.)

Stiva: (to Makhotin and Princess Miaghkaia) Really, Makhotin, you are irritating. The prettiest woman in the world.

Princess Miaghkaia: (furious) Will you dance with me, Stiva?

Stiva: Gladly.

(Stiva and Princess Miaghkaia go off, laughing before the discontented Makhotin. Matvei passes by with a tray of drinks. Makhotin takes a drink and philosophizes.)

Makhotin: To forgetfulness.

Vronsky: (to Anna) Allow me not to waste this exquisite minute with a banal invitation to waltz. Let's talk, shall we?

(The waltz continues as the curtain falls. Vronsky and Anna, absolutely isolated, are talking.

CURTAIN

ACT II

Scene 1

The Tsarkoe Selo race track. At the rise of the curtain, the exclamations of the gamblers and spectators increases gradually, then stops abruptly as the winner crosses the finish line. Some voices are now joyous, others are confused.

First Spectator: Suvarov! Suvarov!

Second Spectator: Lisbeth! Lisbeth!

First Spectator: Suvarov!

Third Spectator: Swell!

First Spectator: Suvarov!

Third Spectator: Swell! Swell!

First Spectator: Suvarov!

Third Spectator: Swell! Swell!

All: Swell! Swell! Swell! Swell! Swell! Bravo!

Third Spectator: Hurrah.

Stiva: Vive Swell!

First Spectator: And I had a hundred rubles on Suvarov.

Third Spectator: Yes, fifteen to one.

Second Spectator: Tom Sterne shows.

First Spectator: (In the enclosure.) Some comfort for not placing first.

Stiva: Yes, in placing. But dangerous on the obstacle if the horse receives nothing.

First Spectator: Go then and collect, you lucky dog.

Second Spectator: I earned five hundred rubles, by my estimate, since it was only ten to one.

Third Spectator: Cord told me right.

Stiva: Yes, from enthusiasm to anguish; there are our masters in the party.

Princess Somatoff: (to Prince Somatoff) I told you so, imbecile!

Prince Somatoff: What? What did you tell me?

Princess Somatoff: That Swell would win.

Prince Somatoff: You told me that? When did you tell me that?

Princess Somatoff: I certainly did. But you never listen to me?

Prince Somatoff: I never listen to you, that's right. But when I win, don't reproach me!

Countess Nordstone: (to Vronsky, who is absorbed with Anna) Do you know who won the race, my dear Count?

Vronsky: (starting, as if from a dream) Countess? The race? But Suvarov, I think. The favorite.

Kitty: Why no, Alexei Vronsky.

Dolly: Suvarov was second. The winner was Swell.

Anna: Swell? Princess Tverskot's horse?

Vronsky: What about that?

Countess Nordstone: If you were a little less absorbed in your discussion, you would have understood without effort the clamors of Swell's supporters. But then! Anna will make you lose sight of everything, as her charm isolates you from the exterior world. Kitty, in your place, I would be jealous! These two act like they are engaged.

Dolly: Ah, Countess, what a singular joke.

(A group at the right, Princess Betsy Tverskaia, Yavshine, Makhotin.)

Makhotin: (rising) Yavshine. We won! Are you coming?

Yavshine: I'm coming. Besides, we are late.

Makhotin: Bah. We're ready! Princess, look at your at your beautiful cousin, Anna Arkadyevna.

Princess Betsy: Well?

Makhotin: She's preventing my friend Vronsky from sensing his duty. He's forgetting he is riding with us in the steeplechase.

Princess Betsy: He's forgetting worse than that.

Makhotin: What else?

Princess Betsy: Oh, oh. All St. Petersburg is talking about it. Every day he's squirreled away with the Karenins. But, not for the husband, nor for his fiancée Kitty Shcherbatskaia.

Makhotin: Come on!

Princess Betsy: Yes, yes! Our virtuous Anna Arkadyevna!

Yavshine: Then, poor Karenin.

Makhotin: Because he's a minister, he's no less a man. Ah! Ah! Ah! But, tell us, Princess, you don't spare your relative.

Princess Betsy: We have fallen out. They are enemies.

Makhotin: In every respect, my friend Vronsky is an imbecile. Are you coming, Yavshine?

Yavshine: Yes. I'm upset. I'm going to see my horse. Excuse me.

(Yavshine leaves by the right.)

Princess Betsy: Why do you think that Vronsky is a fool?

Makhotin: Because this is going too far. I'm sure there's still nothing between Anna Arkadyevna and him. I am his close friend. I know him!

Princess Betsy: The world doesn't have your confidence.

Makhotin: Come on. We live together. He wouldn't be able to hide it from me. To hang around with her for three weeks. But, to seduce a woman—I've tried it—it takes two days siege.

Princess Betsy: Not for every woman.

Makhotin: (laughing) You're right. In general, it takes a lot of time.

Vronsky: (rising, smiling) And, I almost forgot I was in the last race.

Anna: Your trainer Monsieur Cord has come three times to hurry you. You are going to be late.

Vronsky: Bah. I still have twenty good minutes and I prefer not to tire myself before the race.

(Monsieur Cord, the trainer, has approached.)

Vronsky: Well? How is Frou-frou?

Cord: All right, sir! But a little restless. Monsieur M— M—

Vronsky: Makhotin.

Cord: Makhotin. Yes, sir. He's going to walk Gladiator for a half hour. If you ride Gladiator, you might do better.

Vronsky: Oh, thanks! But Frou-frou is nervous. It's more fun to win with a capricious beast than with a tame horse. It's more of a duel.

Anna: A peaceful duel.

Kitty: You won't be in any danger, will you?

Stiva: There's always some danger in a steeplechase. But not for a horseman like Count Alexis Vronsky.

Countess Nordstone: Let's go and take our seats again.

Stiva and Kitty: (turning back together) Not yet!

(Exit Stiva. Anna is the first to regain her sangfroid.)

Countess Nordstone: (to Vronsky, ironically) You don't need to win—a double upset will recompense you.

Vronsky: There's an enigma I'll try to solve during the race—if you will excuse me.

Countess Nordstone: (to Kitty) Are you satisfied with your stay in St. Petersburg, pretty Kitty?

Kitty: Yes, Countess. But, I am a little dull. At first, because I had never been separated from my family before. Certainly Dolly and Stiva were full of care for me and also my great friend, Anna Arkadyevna, but for a young girl, I prefer our Muscovite existence which is more family oriented, less worldly, less shallow.

Dolly: It's true. Existence here is very vain, very pretentious.

Countess Nordstone: I am desolated that you hold this impression of our society.

Anna: But I am sure that my dear Kitty will try with all her heart to improve us when she ties the knot. Soon, right?

Kitty: Oh, nothing is yet definitely fixed. That is to say, the exact date. Isn't that true Count Alexei Kirillovich?

Vronsky: You know very well that on this subject we must follow the wise advice of our parents and the approval of the Emperor.

Kitty: I am afraid. I am a little worried, Alexei, about the influence of your old habits on your resolution which was so joyously taken.

Vronsky: Kitty! Is it possible? It seems to me you are questioning my word as an officer and a gentleman.

Kitty: Is it a question of honor which dictates your present acts, Alexei Kirillovich? I don't accept that.

Vronsky: You know quite well my feelings are the same, always deep.

Kitty: Of course! Of course! Don't say any more and don't listen to them, Alexei Kirillovich.

Countess Nordstone: (to Anna) Look at that. Vronsky and his fiancée are as angry as if they were already married.

(Stiva enters from the right and goes to Vronsky.)

Stiva: Hey! Vronsky!

Dolly: Stiva, don't bet any more; you're spending money without counting. I have many things to buy for the children, and our trip to St. Petersburg has already cost us too much money.

Stiva: Don't worry, you know very well these sacrifices are necessary. Kitty has got to be married well. I will leave you a moment with Anna, if you permit.

Dolly: Of course! I will be with my Kitty, too.

Stiva: Vronsky, you aren't ready? Ladies! Soon you will bet on me during the next race. Vronsky!

(Vronsky goes toward the right. Constantin Levin, center back with his brother, has watched Vronsky leaving. At the moment Stiva seeks to rejoin Vronsky, Levin interposes.)

Levin: Bonjour, Stefan Arkadyevich.

Stiva: The devil take me! Constantin Levin! You, at Tsarkoe Selo, at the races. You must intend to become a man of the world—like your brother Sergei Ivanovich. Good day, subtle psychologist. Your last book was marvelous.

Koznishev: You have read it, Stefan Arkadyevich?

Stiva: No, of course not! But my sister Anna has spoken to me of it. I haven't the time to read it, I am too much absorbed in my work. Come with me, come—I am very happy to see you.

Levin: Where are you intending to take us?

Stiva: I'm running the race with my friend Vronsky! A charming fellow—the fiancé of—oh, I beg your pardon.

Levin: That's all right! That's all right! As you know, Stiva, I should never have indulged in such a dream. I know, I am only a peasant, and he is a brilliant military man who runs obstacle races. I was unable to prevent myself from coming—to see her, perhaps, and to see him, too. It's been too much for me, Stiva.

Stiva: (bored) That's annoying. But, you see, everything is falling into place. But really, I know what I'm saying. There had been something—my good fortune had received something very compromising when you came to see me the last time. You know—I had just given Mademoiselle Roland a kiss. Well, by a sort of miracle, and thanks to my sister Anna, everything is put together again. Dolly is happier than ever, you can quite see.

Levin: Perhaps the quality of our suffering is not the same.

Stiva: Come on! Look a little in that direction. I sacrifice Vronsky to you. You see how I love you with all my heart. I must show you a little singer from the Crystal Palace near the pavilion. I will tell you about her. You didn't wish to greet the princess? She is with my sister, some witty friends and our samovar.

Levin: Your samovar?

Stiva: Yes, that's what we call Countess Lidia Ivanovna. She's always percolating over the most futile subjects. Ah, Ah, come here. No, wait a minute.

(Enter Alexei Karenin.)

Stiva: (to Karenin) Hey! Hey! Karenin! Alexei Alexandrovich, my bear of a brother-in-law. Anna Arkadyevna is here too.

Karenin: Stefan Arkadyevich!

Koznishev: (to his brother) Stiva is, in effect, a very busy man.

Levin: He isn't bad, but—

Stiva: (to Karenin) In fact, brother-in-law, while I hold you for a minute, is it true that there was a meeting of workers in the port of Kronstadt? Pure imagination on the part of the journalists, right? What are they saying in the Imperial Palace?

Karenin: Pardon me, Stefan Arkadyevich—don't raise a question of State in such a place. Suppose some police agent heard my words and reported them, quite twisted, to a prefect who transmitted them to the Emperor. I am a serious man, Stefan Arkadyevich.

Stiva: Naturally, I am also.

Karenin: That's why, I tell you plainly not to speak with me in a place like this of anything but frivolities—for you that won't be very difficult.

Vronsky: (passing by) I present my respects to you Count Karenin.

Karenin: I salute you, Captain.

Vronsky: Excuse me for leaving you a little hastily. But I am riding in the next race.

Karenin: Go, go, sir. Those are the pleasures of your age group.

(Vronsky leaves. A group of ladies pass Karenin.)

Karenin: Ladies, I greet you.

Countess Lidia: Bonjour, Alexei Alexandrovich.

Karenin: (to Anna) You see my tenderness for you is as deep as in those first days, Anna. I left very serious business to spend the end of the day with you.

Anna: I'd appreciate your tenderness better, Alexei, if you didn't always take such care to point out to me each of its manifestations.

Karenin: You're a bit ironical. At these moments you have the facial expression of that fool Stiva.

Anna: My brother is not a fool.

Karenin: He is worse!

Anna: Did you see Seriozha before you left?

Karenin: Yes, he was studying his history lesson with Vassilii Lukich. Also, he told me to kiss you, which I cannot do here, and I regret it.

Anna: That's how you atone for your official tenderness all the time. (to Countess Nordstone and Kitty, who are passing by) Where are you and Kitty off to?

Countess Nordstone: To the betting stalls. We are going to bet on Count Alexei Vronsky, you may be sure.

Kitty: You come too, Anna Arkadyevna.

Anna: No. I prefer staying in my place. I dislike crowds.

Dolly: Me, too. I certainly would not have come if mother hadn't confided Kitty to my care.

Countess Lidia: (to Karenin, who is getting ready to leave) Listen, Alexei Alexandrovich, for the hundredth time, listen to the advice of an old woman. Anna, who I esteem to be a very honest woman, is on dangerous ground. She's finding real pleasure in the conversation of Captain Vronsky, Kitty's fiancé. It is becoming much too serious. Use all your resources to hasten Kitty's marriage, or indeed—

Karenin: Pardon me, my dear friend. You know the extent to which I listen to your sage advice—and in all things, certainly—but here is neither the time nor the place to discuss such a delicate subject.

Countess Lidia: One must subordinate one's acts to the circumstances. I haven't chosen my moment.

Karenin: Well, as for me, my dear friend, I always pick my moments. (laughing) Permit me now to offer you my arm to go to the buffet, if you don't regard me with rancor.

Countess Lidia: How could I?

Karenin: You are a woman!

Countess Lidia: Exactly. Are you leaving Anna alone?

Karenin: Yes. She expressed the desire to come and watch my brother-in-law who's making calf's eyes at the young girl in the cloak room. Ah, one can say that he wastes no time.

(Karenin and Countess Lidia leave towards the buffet.)

Princess Miaghkaia: (who talks to Anna after a moment) You aren't going to bet, Anna Arkadyevna?

Anna: No. I never bet.

Princess Miaghkaia: You are wrong. You miss some very savory sensations.

Anna: I'm just a bourgeois.

(A clock strikes slowly.)

Princess Miaghkaia: Oh! Oh! Excuse me. I have just enough time.

Dolly: I will come with you to the pari-mutuel. I want to watch my husband. You permit me, Anna?

(Dolly and Princess Miaghkaia leave. The Prince and Princess Somatoff: enter. Vronsky enters, unexpectedly, from the left, dressed for the race; he is pale and nervous.)

Princess Somatoff: You should play Fenette this time.

Prince Somatoff: No, Gladiator.

Princess Somatoff: Fenette.

Prince Somatoff: Gladiator.

Princess Somatoff: You just lost one hundred rubles because you wouldn't listen to me. Why won't you bet on Fenette?

Prince Somatoff: Because Major Dimitri is a charming man who gave me this advice at the sea shore.

Princess Somatoff: That doesn't prove Gladiator will win.

Prince Somatoff: Yes! Yes!

Princess Somatoff: No, no, and no. So there!

Anna: (spotting Vronsky) What, is it you?

Vronsky: Yes.

Anna: And the race? And Frou-frou?

Vronsky: I am the last at the weigh-in and they've not started weighing in yet. I have ten minutes ahead of me.

Anna: And you come here, instead of preparing to win?

Vronsky: Yes.

Anna: You seem very nervous!

Vronsky: Indeed, I'm very—anguished. Listen, Anna Arkadyevna, I have resolved, rapidly, just now, to put an end to a dangerous situation.

Anna: Dangerous?

Vronsky: Yes, for three people at least.

Anna: I don't understand you, my friend.

Vronsky: Because you don't wish to understand me.

(Anna is anguished. Time passes.)

Anna: Well—I am listening.

Vronsky: (passing his hand over his face) Yes, soon, after all is forgotten, near you, in the charm of your conversation, and of your presence.

Anna: Vronsky!

Vronsky: A small woman's hand is resting on my arm. Ah, this hand here, it is a call of duty, exacting as my conscience. I am the keeper of the good of this little hand, and suddenly I understood that I cannot keep my word vis-à-vis the young Princess Shcherbatskaia—because of this little hand resting on my arm.

(Anna rises abruptly. Then sits again.)

Anna: Oh, she will die of it.

Vronsky: No, she won't die. She will be ashamed, a great shame for a young girl. One doesn't die of puppy love.

Anna: Then, you don't love Kitty? You played with her young, confiding heart? It's vile! It's cowardly.

Vronsky: I am not master of my fate. At Moscow, in the familial atmosphere, in the monotony of a provincial existence, I sincerely believed I loved her, right up until the day—

Anna: (trying to joke) Up until the day when, coming to St. Petersburg, your comrades, your horses, and your girl friends reclaimed you. Blind, poor blind man who cast aside a real joy for a joy to come; you had only to extend your hand to open your soul to the joy of love.

Vronsky: (very grave) No, Anna, you deceive yourself. I extended my hand towards the only joy, the only love of my life. (he extends his arms towards her and she recoils) And if it is taken from me, with a mysterious face and lowered eyes whose thoughts I cannot read, as you separate yourself from me without looking at me—

Anna: Shut up! Shut up!

Vronsky: Anna!

Anna: Go away. It's a cowardly thing to have spoken where the fear of a public scandal prevents me from protecting myself properly and my honor is at the mercy of a raised voice or glance.

Princess Miaghkaia: (returning) Oh, pardon me if I interfere with you. I am looking for Stiva.

Anna: He must be with the tribunes.

Princess Miaghkaia: Thank you. Excuse me, I am in love

with betting.

(Princess Miaghkaia passes on, laughing with Princess Betsy.)

Anna: (to Vronsky) Go away. Irreparable words have not yet been spoken.

Vronsky: Anna! Here they are! I love you. Do you understand? I love you.

Anna: (triumphant and tragic at the same time) Ah, go! Go! Leave me! I hate you!

Vronsky: You cannot hate me. I have not done anything to deserve your hate.

Anna: Just go!

Vronsky: You must know that on your trip from Moscow to St. Petersburg—that night—in the car carrying us—I sensed—in every fiber that my heart was giving itself to you. It didn't fail to witness itself in even the most banal cordiality, it showed itself to me and all the possibilities of happiness. Anna, in five minutes a clock will strike. And perhaps I won't see you again. Steeplechases are dangerous for those who want them to be dangerous.

Anna: You threaten? I am not afraid!

Vronsky: I threaten only my own life. I know very well it won't move you.

Anna: Mere words!

Vronsky: Yes, before the last act. But, I want to tell you what you have guessed. I love you, I love you, I love you. Nothing else matters—not even my life. If you had been able to love me. We could remake our lives—far from here.

Anna: No. You belong to Kitty. I—I belong to my husband and son—and I don't love you. It's that—the sole, unique reason. I pardon you in the name of what was our confident friendship, for the outrage of your words, for your love. I pardon you for offering to Anna Karenina what your comrades offer to the sad women who accept it—a guilty love, a shabby liaison—this horrible thing they call adultery.

Vronsky: I offer you my whole life! Get divorced, Anna, I love you.

Anna: Shut up, shut up! You have destroyed in one minute all the purity of our reciprocal affection.

Vronsky: Anna, Anna, don't do something violent to yourself. Are you listening to your heart or to your reason?

Anna: My heart, Alexei Kirillovich. I don't love you.

Vronsky: Anna!

Anna: I don't love you!

Vronsky: (recoiling) Ah, well, then! Goodbye, Anna Arkadyevna.

(A clock sounds slowly.)

Vronsky: Goodbye, forever.

Anna: Where are you going?

Vronsky: To race. To race. Goodbye!

Anna: Alexei, listen!

Vronsky: Well?

Anna: Think of Kitty—who loves you.

Vronsky: Adieu!

(Vronsky leaves by the right. Anna, immobile as a statue, watches him go.)

Anna: And yet, I, too, I love you. I love you! I love you!

(Alexei Karenin and Countess Nordstone arrive. Anna sits down very quietly and smiles at them. The clock sounds at a greater distance. The other characters return.)

Countess Lidia: You appear very upset, Anna.

Anna: As a matter of fact, it's the hot air which troubles me a bit. I will watch the race from the tribune. It's better sheltered.

Countess Lidia: (to Karenin) I swear to you, Alexei Alexandrovich, that Vronsky has been with her.

Karenin: Come, come, since Vronsky is running in this race, he couldn't be here at the same time. Do you know, you will end, dear friend, by earning the sobriquet your friends give you of "the Samovar"?

Countess Lidia: From you, it cannot anger me.

(Little by little, groups return, with some preference for the tribune at the right where each takes his measures to follow the race.)

Princess Miaghkaia: I've got Frou-frou for fifty rubles. And you, too, my Kitty? Naturally.

Kitty: Yes, but for much less money.

Dolly: It's true. You are right in every instance.

Anna: (to Karenin) Are you staying with us, near the tribune, Alexei? It's very easy to see the race from here.

Karenin: I didn't come to see the race.

Stiva: (laughing) Just like me; I didn't come to see the ladies!

Karenin: No, to speak the truth, Oblonsky, I didn't come for that reason either.

Anna: You are crazy, Stiva. Dolly's only two steps away.

Stiva: Bah! She has such confidence in me.

Karenin: (ironically to Anna) You were right before. Stiva is not a fool.

Princess Somatoff: (standing on a chair, looking at the track) Well! What did I tell you? Look, my Fenette! What a pretty filly.

Prince Somatoff: Yes, you're looking at the rider.

Princess Somatoff: And your Gladiator! You are going to

see—a nanny goat.

Prince Somatoff: Evidently Lieutenant Makhotin pleases you less.

Princess Somatoff: Yes. He's a guard of the Empress.

(Constantin Levin and his brother Sergei Koznishev appear.)

Koznishev: What pleasure can you find in this sort of feast, Constantin? There's plenty of open ground where one can mingle with those who don't work—an entire society which smells of perfume and not a Mouzhik in sight.

Levin: To be sure, Sergei, I am not here for my pleasure, but to purge a dream from my heart. Irrevocably.

Koznishev: Ah, you're indeed amorous, poor Constantin, although you speak like a poet.

Levin: It's true. I speak and you write.

Stiva: (to Princess Miaghkaia) When I am by myself, separated from you by ten meters, I find myself disoriented.

Princess Miaghkaia: Then go to the cloak room where there is a very pretty person who said to me: "Pouah to back door lovers." You are no better than your friend Makhotin.

Stiva: Ah, slander! I will go find your cloak so as to slide a letter in the pocket. Don't make me say any more.

Princess Miaghkaia: Liar. My cloak! A letter for me. A letter with ten rubles, yes, for the cloak room lady.

Stiva: You are exquisite. One can hide nothing from you. I am going to sit near you just the same.

Princess Miaghkaia: If you wish. You are what they call in France a coquette.

Stiva: Detestable joke.

Prince Somatoff: Oh, look! The horses are breaking into a gallop!

Princess Betsy: Oh, Gladiator, the pretty beast.

Countess Lidia: (to Anna, who is to her left on the stand) How nervous Captain Vronsky seems. Don't you think so, Anna?

Anna: I hadn't noticed, Lidia Ivanovna.

General: (to Karenin, whom he has taken by the arm) Grotesque! Useless! Dangerous to risk his skin on the green turf. It's energy stolen from the Emperor.

Karenin: Danger is an indispensable element. That's important for officers. The sport has a profound feeling. It is irritating that we only see the superficial side of it.

General: Very pretty, all that, my dear Minister, but then—why don't you race?

Karenin: My race is of a more difficult type.

General: Bravo! Very deep! Well, as for me, I am in a

bad humor with the races because I am too fat. That's the truth. I am a frank person.

Prince Somatoff: (counting the horses) Fourteen, fifteen, sixteen and seventeen. Exactly seventeen officers in the race. This will be a very beautiful steeplechase.

Stiva: There will be some surprises.

Countess Nordstone: Oh, the horse of Lieutenant Yavshine seems like a grasshopper.

Stiva: (laughing) That will serve him well in the jumps.

Karenin: (to General) The Emperor takes a lively interest in the sport. Soon he's going to be here.

General: So that's why there's such a crowd! But we know quite well

First Spectator: Come, come over here. We can see better.

A Lady: Are they already on line for the start?

Second Spectator: Good! A captain thrown from his saddle.

Stiva: It's an Infantry Captain! That will teach him.

Koznishev: (to Levin and Alexei Karenin) My Minister, I am happy to present my respects to you.

General: Excuse me, gentlemen, but it's my custom to be at the buffet during these spectacles.

Karenin: Go, go, General, and get thinner.

General: I am going to continue my diet.

(In the distance, fanfares, trumpets, followed by the clamor of the crowd.)

Some Voices: (distant) The Emperor! The Emperor! The Emperor has come! Hurrah!

Levin: (to Karenin) Why aren't you in the imperial box? You, a Minister.

Karenin: Those are for the Grand Dukes.

(More fanfares.)

Levin: Here the arrival of the Emperor makes less of an impression than down there, listen.

Karenin: (smiling) They see him in the distance.

Koznishev: You are very skeptical in all things!

Karenin: No, but the crowd is poor and amuses itself at the races. The Emperor becomes part of that spectacle and the crowd acclaims him. Here the race is the main thing. It's the clan of gamblers. The Emperor irritates them the most. He delays the departure of the horses in the race. And then, our loyalty doesn't applaud him—it suffers him.

Koznishev: How much of your observation is original?

Stiva: It's the devil to line up seventeen horses.

Koznishev: The starter is very inept.

Gambler: By God, he is Russian. What's needed is an Englishman. Come on, come on. Let them go. He could easily give the signal.

A Lady: Watch Gladiator.

Second Gambler: Star wants to start too soon, inept brute, imbecile. It's the Lieutenant of Hussars who's making his horse nervous. Ah, no. Let's go! Let's go!

Karenin: (smiling) That's one of the essential duties of the riding class—lining up horses.

Levin: Go on. I might, perhaps, make a good romantic novelist.

Koznishev: Rather an excellent psychologist. Your field of observation is so vast and your faculties so penetrating.

Stiva: There they go!

(Lengthy murmurs from the crowd which takes a passionate interest in the spectacle. The clock of departure rings slowly. The last bettors return from the betting booths to watch the race.)

Stiva: (watching the first jump) Attention! The jump! Hoopla!

Kitty: Brava, Frou-frou.

Gamblers: It's poorly done. He lost his stirrup. Hands down. Hurrah! Bravo! Bravo, Makhotin! There's a bump in the earth. He's made a mistake! Ah!

Crowd: Oh, oh!

(In the tribunes, a woman screams.)

First Gambler: A rider has fallen.

Second Gambler: It's Major Kouslov.

Karenin: It's Countess Nordstone who screamed. We know why, don't we, gentlemen?

Koznishev: If we followed the race with our glasses.

Karenin: We could follow it better here, turning our backs.

Koznishev: In turning our backs?

Karenin: Absolutely.

Koznishev: How's that?

Gambler: Frou-frou's in the lead!

Princess Somatoff: The last! Your horse is the last!

Kitty: Yes, yes, Frou-frou!

Gamblers: Bravo, Vronsky! What madness. He's going to kill his horse! Use the whip, Makhotin, use the whip.

Karenin: Absolutely! On the faces of the spectators, and wait, it's an attempt at observation which I give you gratis for your next novel. There are seventeen officers in the race, all celebrated, all brilliant riders, the most choice, and not one who has not a flirt or a mistress in this elegant gathering. You get my method?

Koznishev: It must be very up to date.

Karenin: I am: from taste and profession—

Gamblers: Frou-frou's losing ground. Gladiator gained five lengths. Ten lengths.

Stiva: Star's back in the running. Use the bridle, Dimitri, use the bridle.

Levin: (to his brother) See how Kitty Shcherbatskaia trembles for her Vronsky.

Koznishev: Anna also appears troubled. I will end by believing what they say.

Levin: What are they saying?

Koznishev: The husband! Hush!

Princess Miaghkaia: Bravo, Makhotin.

Karenin: You see, indeed, gentlemen. My method was foolproof. Besides, look how the Princess Miaghkaia is radiant. She is very much the friend, I believe, of Lieutenant Makhotin.

Stiva: (laughing) It's Gladiator who's in the lead.

Gamblers: Frou-frou is finished! The whip, Vronsky, the whip! Fenette is last. Harrah, Makhotin.

Karenin: And Lieutenant Makhotin rides Gladiator. You see!

Koznishev: Bravo! This is marvelous.

Levin: I find the game a little immoral.

Karenin: Bah! Our so called immorality of observation depends on their real immorality. There's Princess Somatoff, who appears a little nervous to me.

Voice: (in the distance) Fall! At the stream!

Karenin: Major Dimitri of the Guard on Fenette.

Gamblers: Frou-frou's coming on strong! They near the little woods! Dimitri! Thief! Clumsy! He did it on purpose. Yes, yes, he's fallen on purpose. Fenette is without a rider.

Stiva: She's going to annoy Frou-frou.

Gamblers: It's abominable. There are three riders out of the race, injured. Dangerously, perhaps. What barbarism! Delicious barbarism which you enjoy like a cruel cat lapping stolen milk.

Countess Nordstone: Me, I am enjoying it! I am.

Dolly: (to Kitty) Be calm, dear. He's an excellent horseman! Have confidence!

Karenin: Eh, well, Sergei Ivanovich. Isn't it as good as living a good novel?

Koznishev: Talk of drama! For even here's my brother

Constantin, who is suffering a thousand deaths to see young Princess Shcherbatskaia suffering for her fiancé who's in the race.

Karenin: It is true! The purest love has the same expressions as the other kind.

Stiva: Gladiator! Gladiator!

Gamblers: No, Frou-frou! Runs beautiful. He's lost his stirrups! It's a mad fury! It's a duel to the death! She's passing, she's passing. She's ahead. Bravo! Frou-frou!

Stiva: Bravo!

Gamblers: Bravo, Vronsky!

Stiva: She's won!

Gamblers: Watch out for the stream. Look out, Vronsky! Frou-frou! Frou-frou!

Kitty and Anna: (crying out at the same time) Oh! Oh!

Karenin: Eh! What's this mean?

(Great tumult in the tribunes and corridors. Kitty faints. Anna cries without constraint while the majority of the public follows the race with growing anguish.)

Karenin: His horse has fallen on him!

Stiva: Vronsky has fallen.

Anna: Stiva, Stiva! Tell me he is not injured!

Karenin: In heaven's name, Anna, shut up!

Anna: (without hearing him) Stiva! Stiva! Please, tell me he is not injured!

Countess Lidia: (to Karenin) What an abominable scandal this will cause. Get her out of here.

Karenin: Anna, Anna. I order you to follow me.

Anna: (recognizing her husband) God! Now I am lost!

(They crowd around Kitty, who has fainted. Karenin pulls Anna, who wants to run off and is listening to the words of Princess Betsy. Karenin holds her.)

Karenin: No public scandal! Come.

(Anna follows him, weeping loudly. The gamblers' tumult continues until the curtain at the end of the scene.)

Gamblers: (with an intensity that keeps mounting until the end of the scene) Yavshine has fallen. Vronsky doesn't get up. Gladiator is in the lead. Frou-frou is hit. Two riders on the ground again. Gladiator! Gladiator! Gladiator! Bravo! Bravo! More than seven horses in the race. Ha, ha, Gladiator. Gladiator, Gladiator!

Stiva: Hurrah! I win a thousand rubles.

Countess Nordstone: But, Vronsky! Vronsky!

Gamblers: Gladiator! Gladiator! Gladiator! Gladiator! Gladiator! Gladiator!

CURTAIN

ACT II

Scene 2

Alexei Karenin's office. At the rise of the curtain, Seriozha slides furtively into the room and hides under his father's desk.

Seriozha: Hee, hee.

Vassilii's Voice: Seriozha Alexeivitch. Monsieur Seriozha.

Seriozha: Hee, hee.

Vassilii: (entering) What? In spite of His Excellency forbidding you, you dare to come and amuse yourself in his office? Where are you, villainous little devil? Come on, answer your tutor.

Seriozha: Hee, hee.

Vassilii: Ah, there you are! Well, suppose now that the Minister and Anna Arkadyevna return from the races and find you here. Who will be reprimanded? Me, without a doubt.

Seriozha: Bah! It's only five o'clock. The races aren't finished yet.

Vassilii: Monsieur Seriozha.

Seriozha: And we risk nothing, playing all over the house.

Vassilii: You think so? We, at least, risk feeling guilty.

Seriozha: What's guilt?

Vassilii: We risk even more. Alas, as I predicted—

(Alexei Karenin arrives unexpectedly, followed by Anna.)

Karenin: What's this mean, Vassilii Lukich? You and Seriozha in my cabinet?

Vassilii: Excellency, you see me desolated.

Karenin: Tell me the real reason, without embellishment.

Vassilii: Well, His Excellency, Seriozha Alexeivitch, after his lesson, wanted to play hide and seek and he just got here.

Karenin: Did you remind him that his entry here was forbidden?

Vassilii: But—

Karenin: Answer!

Seriozha: Yes, Papa, Vassilii did remind me.

Karenin: And you disobeyed him?

Seriozha: Yes, Papa. It's not his fault we are here.

Karenin: You admit that you alone are guilty?

Seriozha: Yes, Papa.

Karenin: You will then be the only one punished.

Anna: Oh, Alexei! He has so graciously admitted his fault.

Karenin: Good manners after a mistake do not excuse it. The guilty must be punished.

Seriozha: It's nothing, Mama, don't cry.

Anna: My dear.

Karenin: Would you kindly accompany Seriozha to his room, Vassilii Lukich? He will dine alone this evening.

Vassilii: As you wish, Excellency.

Anna: My little Seriozha.

Seriozha: Mama?

Anna: Hug me!

Seriozha: Oh! Yes, Mama.

(Vassilii Lukich and Seriozha leave. Anna continues to cry silently. Karenin walks up and down, nervously.)

Karenin: (abruptly) I beg you to cease crying instantly. From this moment, no useless tears; remember to what extent tears exasperate and upset me.

Anna: That doesn't matter at all. I know, in spite of all, I will receive no indulgence from you.

Karenin: Before speaking of indulgence, let's concern ourselves with justice. I don't know everything. I am listening to you.

Anna: What do you want to know? It isn't a question of confessing; I have nothing to confess.

Karenin: You made me ridiculous just now.

Anna: I believe in having feelings besides those some ridicule.

Karenin: Don't jest! You manifested an anguish at Captain Vronsky's fall that only a spouse or mistress could dare to show. Do you deny it?

Anna: I will not deny the evidence.

Karenin: You admit you are the mistress of Captain Vronsky?

Anna: I did not say that. I haven't said anything which isn't true.

Karenin: You are frank. I am ready to believe your word if you will swear to me.

Anna: I swear it.

Karenin: It is then absolutely infuriating that you have created that impression before the world today.

Anna: That is, then—the most serious aspect—

Karenin: Would you expect me to ask reparation from Captain Vronsky for an injury he didn't commit?

Anna: I think I ought to be asked.

Karenin: That's fair. Pardon me. (a pause) I've always felt so strong morally and my spirit of justice is such that I never dreamed I could be placed in such a cruel situation. I suffer greatly.

Anna: Alexei—

Karenin: I suffer—from your fault. It is just that you suffer in your turn. I have nothing to reproach myself with.

Anna: You want everything to be resolved by the logic of your reasoning?

Karenin: I owe it to myself.

Anna: You have no heart, Alexei Alexandrovich!

Karenin: I have a conscience, Anna! It has and always will dictate my conduct. Does Vronsky love you?

Anna: Yes.

Karenin: He told you so?

Anna: Yes.

Karenin: And you—love him?

Anna: I only realized I loved him today.

Karenin: Ah! Excuse me, one doesn't learn such news without emotion, when one has long had the impression of serenity and happiness.

Anna: Alexei—

(A pause.)

Karenin: Have you thought about what you could do at present?

Anna: Yes, Alexei. It would be loyal—honest, to separate without scandal. We no longer ought to be husband and wife.

Karenin: (violently) Divorce! Ah, ah—never that!

Anna: Why not?

Karenin: Because, once free, you will marry the man you love! Because you will be happy and he will be happy. Happy at my expense. Ah, never that—a thousand times no! You are my wife by law. You will remain my wife.

(A knock at the door.)

Karenin: What is it?

Voice: A dispatch for you, sir.

Karenin: (going to the door and opening it slightly) Give it to me. Thanks. (closing door, to Anna) You will allow me— (reading) Ah! (throwing the dispatch on his desk and pausing) Pardon me, the violence of my words— first because violence is never helpful in a discussion and then because I envisage something henceforth impossible. I have just received news of Count Alexei Vronsky.

Anna: What?

Karenin: Well— (gesturing)

Anna: He is dead. Oh, oh! (she swoons into Karenin's arms) It's I. I am responsible for his death.

Karenin: Anna!

Anna: Yes, I killed him. I killed him. He died from despair.

Karenin: How can that be?

Anna: Earlier today, before mounting his horse, he came to me to tell me of his love. Never before had he spoken of it to me, I swear it. And I—I replied that I did not love him. I told him to marry Kitty. And then he left— like a fool—and now he's killed himself. He killed himself because he thought I didn't love him.

Karenin: Calm yourself, Anna. Calm yourself. I know you are a loyal creature.

Anna: Yes, Alexei. I struggled with all my strength. Forgive him, he is dead. You cannot remain angry with the dead. I understand the courage I will need.

Karenin: You will console yourself, Anna, in the foyer, near your son, our little Seriozha; you are not without fault, but you are not guilty. You will leave tonight for the country with little Seriozha. There, in isolation, you will regain peace in your heart, and when you do you will also regain your husband, who knows how to love you. You agree to this?

Anna: Yes, yes.

Karenin: You promise to do just as I have decided?

Anna: Yes, yes.

Karenin: You will leave this evening with your son?

Anna: Yes.

Karenin: Without seeing anyone, without speaking to anyone about what has happened?

(Anna is crying on her husband's shoulder. She casts a glance at the fatal dispatch. Suddenly her expression changes. She pushes Karenin and seizes the paper.)

Anna: You lied to me! He is alive.

Karenin: Anna—

Anna: Captain Vronsky only fainted. I pardon you your abominable lie for the joy this gives me.

Karenin: Unfortunate woman!

Anna: Happy woman. Because I love him and he loves me. Thanks to you, my lord and master. You have torn my scruples from me. Ah, you cleverly planned your frightful trick to discover if I had been his mistress—or if I had been true to you. Oh, a clever diplomatic noose—and a complete profanation.

Karenin: Have you so clearly understood?

Anna: And you, you have never understood me. You, who for many years lived near me, carrying on with your mistress, expecting me to follow your example, your advice. There's your wife and your mistress—and your method, your superiority. Your cold look is not going to rekindle any love for you in my eyes! Now comes love, great, immense, the sole love of my life; I struggled as an honest woman against my own forces. I brought to despair the man that I love and who loved me to the point of committing suicide—and you let me think him dead so as to know the depth of my feeling and to impose on me a course of action that would make you feel comfortable! In truth, Alexei Alexandrovich, I knew you were diplomatic, but not until such a lie—

Karenin: And—what do you propose to do now?

Anna: To separate from you.

Karenin: I already told you why I won't divorce. My reasons are greater than before. I don't intend for you to marry your accomplice.

Anna: You insult me; he is not my lover.

Karenin: As long as I live, he will never be your husband.

Anna: Then we will be simply free from one another since the law is in the service of your unswerving will.

Karenin: It's not only man's law in my camp; there's also the moral law.

Anna: Moral law is against lying! You lied to me just

now!

Karenin: Who are you to blame me? In an organized society, the most elevated ought to be an example. We must remain examples! My duty today, despite the fact I've learned, this sad fact, is to point out to you the ruin which will follow from a mad act on your part. My career, our situation, will collapse under this ridicule. Never! I don't deserve it! I won't accept it!

Anna: You are right, my freedom will be a catastrophe.

Karenin: Understand me! It is impossible for you not to return, from conscience, to your duty, to society and to me. Are you listening to me, Anna?

Anna:
Yes, yes. I am listening.

Karenin: We cannot divorce, you understand? I say so. I don't wish it. I repeat—we cannot.

Anna: Indeed. Such a scandal.

Karenin: It won't be. I am happy at this return to reason, Anna. You return to yourself. Thank you, and I now regret having provoked such storms just now, which are all so hateful to me after your admission—and for which I remain solely responsible.

Anna: I know you prefer gentleness and I give you credit for such gentleness.

Karenin: All that there is, is justice—a justice due—without reserve to your fidelity. Well, I ask you to finish with a single blow this sad subject and to decide, from today, what is to be done. Captain Vronsky doesn't know that you love him. It is preferable that he never know it. The incident earlier at the races may pass unperceived. Will you promise me never to see him again?

Anna: (fiercely) No!

Karenin: Anna!

Anna: (sitting down) How to promise you such a thing! We are exposed to each other every day. The scandal would be as visible to the world if you don't receive him without having a valid reason than if I ran away with him.

Karenin: Anna!

Anna: Then, I ask you, in my turn, to what point are we going, since we are to remain husband and wife? What is the solution you offer me?

Karenin: Wait.

Anna: Wait! So I can become his mistress! That might be tomorrow, tonight, immediately. What must be done, must be done now. Decide quickly, Alexei.

Karenin: The circumstances do not inspire me. I cannot make decisions in the face of a fait accompli.

Anna: I love him! Is that a fait accompli?

Karenin: If I let you commit this irreparable madness today, it will be shame and disgust for yourself and your love, and everyone's scorn, then you will find your life on the margin of society.

Anna: But, what do you offer me in exchange? A façade of virtue and a heart full of lies to be your wife and to be your enemy? Stay for the world and the Court, Anna Karenina, a good wife and good mother, and here at home, adultery, hypocrisy, odious to you—and especially to myself. Your spirit of justice admits this rather than a separation? I cannot debase myself to that degree, Alexei. I will not be your accomplice!

Karenin: You cannot leave, Anna. You don't belong to this man.

Anna: He loves me—and I love him. You are not going to stop our destinies.

Karenin: I will employ with you the methods that must be used against a harlot or such women. I will care for you as they care for mad women, with a straightjacket, if necessary. And I will break your pride and your love, because I will it.

Anna: I am not afraid!

Karenin: As for him—I swear to you—he will disappear.

Anna: You are going to kill him?

Karenin: Anna!

Anna: Oh, properly, within the law, without a doubt, by sending him to some distant butchery for God and the Emperor. You are a Minister, he is a soldier, he will obey. Unless you provoke him right away and kill him yourself. Fight—tomorrow! Kill him. Do it openly. But not with false dispatches, nor with political pretexts. But, perhaps you are afraid!

(Karenin passes his hand in front of his face very coldly. He opens the door at the right.)

Karenin: (pointing) Go to your man! You are free!

(Anna is stupefied by this development. Obeying her husband's glance, she leaves. The door remains open. After she disappears, Karenin, with an indefinable smile goes to the door.)

Karenin: (calling) Vassilii, Vassilii!

(Karenin goes to the window and watches.)

Vassilii: (entering) Excellency.

Karenin: My son, bring him right away.

Vassilii: Yes, Excellency. (exits)

Karenin: (alone at window) No carriage about. That's good.

(Hearing the noise of a door closing, Karenin struggles and opens the window. Seriozha enters from the door.)

Seriozha: Papa!

Karenin: Come here. To the balcony. What do you see on the street in front of our door?

Seriozha: A woman. It's Mama!

Karenin: Call to her.

Seriozha: Mama! She's turning. Mama!

(Seriozha sends Anna some kisses.)

Karenin: Call again.

Seriozha: Mama!

(Noise of a door closing. Karenin closes the window and taking Seriozha by the hand, leads him to the door at the right.)

Karenin: Sit still.

Seriozha: (very gay) Mama!

Anna: (off) Seriozha!

(Karenin releases Seriozha who stays happily at center stage. Karenin steps to the door. Anna reenters like a mad woman, arms extended towards her son.)

Anna: My treasure!

(Anna is totally lost. She holds Seriozha in her arms. She sobs uncontrollably.)

Anna: My dear, my son! My Seriozha. My love.

(Karenin closes the door and goes over to Anna and Seriozha.)

Karenin: You see clearly, Anna, that you cannot leave.

CURTAIN

ACT III

Venice. Main hall of an old Renaissance Palazzo. Anna is seated in front of a sort of loggia at the back. She is in profile. Vronsky is painting her portrait. Golenishchev is stretched on a divan. The noise of the oars of a gondola is heard passing and the gondolier is singing.

Gondolier: Ho, hi! Ho! La! La! La! La! Ho! Hi ho!

(The voice and the sound of the oars slowly die away.)

Golenishchev: It's pretty, isn't it?

Vronsky: What?

Golenishchev: (embracing the entire decor in a gesture) All this! Venice, the misty water of the canals, the gondoliers who sing the old romantic songs of love and Romeo and Juliet.

Vronsky: (irritated) Golenishchev!

Golenishchev: Have you got some cigarettes?

Vronsky: Yes. There, on the chimney, in the big box.

Golenishchev: (opening the box) Care for one?

Vronsky: Yes, thanks.

Golenishchev: Would you like to smoke, Madame?

Anna: (smiling) Merci, no. I am not a true Russian. I've never cared to smoke.

Golenishchev: Then, truly, it's decided? You are leaving for Naples in eight days?

Anna: Irrevocably. Right, Aloysha?

Vronsky: Yes, yes. We've had enough of canals and sleeping under the Adriatic sun and the Tower of Saint Mark. Two months of humidity! Brrr! We are heading south.

Golenishchev: That sounds quite gay. What will I do, left all to myself?

Vronsky: Whatever you were doing before we arrived. After two or three years in exile, you must be accustomed to solitude. There's something to do every day, you have a pliant enough character. Tomorrow, who knows? You may meet a Muscovite family.

Golenishchev: I don't believe it, Vronsky. Few of our compatriots are willing to pass company with a democrat expelled from Russia for being subversive.

Anna: Here! Here in Venice!

Golenishchev: Precisely. Civic courage is not a very widespread virtue.

Anna: (laughing) Then we are heroes, Vronsky.

Golenishchev: Oh, you two! It's not the same thing. You are not married. You are irregulars.

Anna: (rising, very pale) Pardon me, Aloysha. I'm a little tired. I need to rest.

Vronsky: And the portrait? Are you going?

Anna: A little later, a little later. Excuse me.

(Anna leaves by way of the loggia.)

Golenishchev: She's rather fantastic, your comrade, but one can overlook little things. She's a model fit for a king.

Vronsky: Enough! I am angry to be obliged to tell you, but you are lacking in tact with regard to her. I love her. She is my wife before God and she is to everyone Countess Vronsky, and I demand that you consider her as such, you from whom we have hidden nothing.

Golenishchev: That's fine. Don't be angry.

Vronsky: I am not angry. I merely explain to you. I had to resign to leave with her. I love her above all things. We left Russia because it was impossible for us to live there like husband and wife. The world kept us apart because of the cruelty of Karenin, who, although aware of our love, would never agree to a divorce.

Golenishchev: Right, right, my dear comrade. You are happy, that's the essential thing. You know me. I am a philosopher. One doesn't need to furnish me with explanations. You've known me since college. I have always been so.

Vladimir: (entering) My Captain?

Vronsky: What is it?

Vladimir: The agent is here with someone who wishes to look at the palazzo to rent.

Anita: (entering after Vladimir) Si, Signour! Il Signour Campanetti and une bellissima signora—

Vronsky: (aside, to Golenishchev) Ah, the devil! And no way to avoid them. (aloud) Anita, the Countess is in her room. Go tell her that someone is going to visit the palazzo and also tell her that I am going to leave with Golenishchev.

Anita: Bien, Excellenza.

Vronsky: And you, Vladimir, you can tell Campanetti that we are going to leave the place. Go, why are you waiting?

Vladimir: My Captain.

Vronsky: You have something to tell me?

Vladimir: I believe the lady who wishes to rend the palazzo is Russian.

Vronsky: Well, what is so astonishing about that? Does that please you?

Vladimir: Oh yes, my Captain.

Vronsky: Well, so much the better! March at present, my boy.

(Vladimir leaves.)

Golenishchev: Another one who misses his country.

Vronsky: (going towards the gallery) Come this way, will you? We will avoid our compatriot by leaving this way.

Golenishchev: Speaking of compatriots, General Serpukhovskoy arrived in Venice yesterday. Do you know him?

Vronsky: Do I know him? We were cadets together. He's gone a long way. Are you coming?

(Vronsky leaves.)

Golenishchev: (shouting) I am going to bring your cigarettes. I have no more Russian tobacco.

(No response. Golenishchev methodically fills his cigarette cases with cigarettes, lights one, goes to the door and disappears as Princess Miaghkaia comes in with Campanetti.)

Princess Miaghkaia: Was that gentleman the actual owner of the palazzo?

Campanetti: No, Excellenza. He's a parasite, a Russian nihilist. The actual owner is—

Princess Miaghkaia: Fine. I won't ask any more. What room is this that we are in?

Campanetti: This is the grand reception hall of the Palazzo del Signour Bragadinio, Senator of the Republic of Venice in the seventeenth century. The palazzo was built for him, but he died of natural causes, after having left all his fortune to the illustrious Chevalier Casanova de Seingalt, celebrated for his escape from the Piombi and a thousand other admirable and superior things.

Princess Miaghkaia: (irritated) What became of it then?

Campanetti: Then, the Signour Casanova de Seingalt sold one by one all the chief art works the Senator Bragadinio had here. He only kept the frescos in the ceiling—which are still here. Watch your head, Signora, because he couldn't take them away. Ha, ha, ho. Here is a masterpiece of Carpaccio, a very illustrious Venetian painter who pictures the Archangel Saint George knocking down a dangerous dragon.

(Fatigued by this verbosity, Princess Miaghkaia is looking over the furniture. She has come to Vronsky's easel with Anna's portrait. She lets out a cry of astonishment.)

Princess Miaghkaia: Well, for goodness' sake!

Campanetti: No, no. This is a crudity of an amateur painter. The Carpaccio is over here.

Princess Miaghkaia: But, this portrait isn't finished. Who painted it?

Campanetti: Pooh! The tenant of the palazzo, a Count, very rich. It's the portrait of his wife. She's a Russian Excellenza.

Princess Miaghkaia: What's his name?

Campanetti: Count Vronsky. Former Captain in the Imperial Guard.

Princess Miaghkaia: Ah, Vronsky, it's unheard of!

Campanetti: You know the Signor?

Princess Miaghkaia: Yes, I know him. He's an old friend.

Campanetti: He is here with his wife, a bellissima Excellenza.

Princess Miaghkaia: But, he's not married! Still! Yes, with his wife. I know, I know. Will you tell them I am here?

Campanetti: Ah!

Princess Miaghkaia: Tell them immediately.

Campanetti: (loud) Anita! Anita! (to Princess Miaghkaia) Don't tell him I'll let you have the palazzo for one thousand a month. He pays two thousand. (Anita enters) Tell the Contessa immediately that a lady wishes to see her. (low) Tell her not to say she's paying five hundred a month, this lady will pay one thousand.

(Anita leaves)

Campanetti: You understand. The season is over. I've been able to get this enormous price reduction from the—

Princess Miaghkaia: Fine. Fine. Will you leaven me and wait for me below?

Campanetti: And then, if they are not married, because the owner of the palazzo is an apostolic proto-notary. I am not sorry to see them leave. You understand?

Anita: (returning) The Contessa is coming now.

Campanetti: I'll go down with you, Anita.

(Campanetti and Anita leave, talking with animation. A pause. Anna enters.)

Anna: Madame? Ah, Nadine Miaghkaia!

Princess Miaghkaia: Good day. You weren't expecting my visit today.

Anna: What a surprise! And what luck!

Princess Miaghkaia: Indeed, miraculous luck. I just arrived in Venice yesterday. I intend to stay some months. And now, in the first apartment to rent that I visit, I see the unfinished portrait of my friend, Anna Karenina.

Anna: (upset) Nadine, my dear, don't give me that name. Here, to all, I am the Countess Vronsky.

Princess Miaghkaia: I know, I know. Pardon me, Anna. I am excusable. I wasn't in Saint Petersburg when you left and I've been badly informed about you and Vronsky. I only knew, in general, of the break with Kitty.

Anna: Poor little Kitty.

Princess Miaghkaia: She has been very, very sick. But at present, she is cured and Constantin Levin, whom I don't like, appears to me ready to marry her.

Anna: May she be happy. My God, I don't wish her any

harm.

Princess Miaghkaia: I know, Anna. Love is a terrible master. One can do nothing about it—and sometimes it grows among the ruins.

Anna: Your indulgence touches me, Nadine.

Princess Miaghkaia: Not for a minute have I stopped pitying you and admiring you, Anna! I have always uncovered the truth in all the gossip. I was in the Crimea and Yalta when the news of your departure began to spread. I will let you imagine what became of such an event at a distance and in the milieu of a frivolous fashionable beach society—all the sympathies of the Saint Petersburg crowd were with your husband, this glacial man who has never understood you. What made undertaking your defense difficult was Kitty's illness, for which you cannot be held responsible, and the abandonment of your son, about which I did take your part. Your son was thirteen years old and no longer a baby demanding maternal care every minute. He was a little man, intelligent, healthy and completely educated.

(From the moment that the Princess mentioned Seriozha, Anna was hardly able to contend with her emotion. She now speaks in a voice totally changed.)

Anna: Don't go on, Nadine. It's a question of conscience that concerns no one but me and which no one needs to plead.

Princess Miaghkaia: My intention was not to cause you pain. My intention was only to prove how well I understood you.

Anna: Thank you, thank you. (a pause) Vronsky will deeply regret having missed your visit.

Princess Miaghkaia: But we shall see each other again. You aren't going immediately?

Anna: No. Not immediately.

Princess Miaghkaia: I will have great pleasure in seeing him! And our dear Stiva—have you had news of him often? What a charming companion, isn't he?

Anna: Dolly writes me often. There are only a few people with whom I remain in correspondence.

Princess Miaghkaia: What! Nobody writes you news of Saint Petersburg?

Anna: Matrona, my old nurse writes me every month. "Your son is doing fine, Anna Arkadyevna." And that suffices for me—almost.

Princess Miaghkaia: (eagerly) Then, you don't know? You hear nothing from Alexei Karenin?

Anna: Nothing.

Princess Miaghkaia: The newspapers must have told you he is no longer Minister. But what they don't say is that our Samovar, Lidia Ivanovna, has taken a high hand in his house. Imagine a directress of conscience—and it has resulted in some strange doings in your home. Everything is preoccupied with God and the saints of religion. There is a kind of frenzy to everything between them; there's an amusing, pious pretext to hide the reality of this relationship. (silence) Apparently, this leaves you cold—and you are correct. When are you leaving this palazzo?

Anna: In five or six days, I think.

Princess Miaghkaia: Good, then I will finish the visit tomorrow. It's getting late. I am so talkative. Will Vronsky still be glad to see me? We shall come, Alexander and I, at five p.m.

Anna: Nadine!

Princess Miaghkaia: Yes?

Anna: Who is Alexander?

Princess Miaghkaia: Oh, you are not au courant? Alexander Ivanovich, my friend, is a great composer whom I love. We are in Venice for a kind of honeymoon. I dare say that Alexander and Vronsky and you and I, will make a perfect quartet.

Anna: Nadine.

Princess Miaghkaia: How stupid I've been. You're upset that I haven't told you everything. But everybody knows we split up, Makhotin and me. Oh my dear, he was impossible. You will see that Alexander is quite different—and what an artist! You will be crazy for hours after having seen him.

Anna: I don't think—

Princess Miaghkaia: You will see. You will see. Until tomorrow.

Anna: Tomorrow we are going to go out, and I'm not sure—

Princess Miaghkaia: After tomorrow then, whenever you wish.

Anna: I'd like it better and Vronsky also, without a doubt, not to meet—

Princess Miaghkaia: You don't wish to receive us?

Anna: You, Nadine, very willingly, but this gentleman—

Princess Miaghkaia: He's the man I love! And I don't understand your reticence at all. Especially on your part, in your situation. I love him the way you love Vronsky. We travel together the way you travel with Vronsky, but he is free and I am a widow. Vronsky was engaged and you were married, you have a strange idea of which of the two of us ought to be more proud! You don't wish to receive us? You, you frequent every day, here even, men who are worth nothing. Nihilists! Ah, ah, you don't wish to receive us!

Anna: It's just not possible.

(Anna rings.)

Princess Miaghkaia: Then adieu, Anna. I regret having defended you so well—and from today I will do as everyone else (Anita enters) and give all my sympathy to your husband, Count Alexei Karenin, and my tears for the son you have abandoned.

Anna: Escort this lady out, Anita.

(Princess Miaghkaia leaves very quickly.)

Anita: Santa Madonna! An abandoned son?

Anna: I told you to escort this lady.

(Anita leaves. Anna remains, quite pale, before the entrance to the loggia.)

Anna: She's right. Which of us ought to be more proud?

(Vronsky approaches softly.)

Vronsky: Take me into your dream.

Anna: My dear!

(Anna puts her hands on Vronsky's shoulders and looks longingly into his eyes.)

Anna: Do you love me?

Vronsky: With all my heart! All my thoughts are of you.

Anna: You must love me without reticence, without measure. When I feel myself carried away, as in a torrent of passion, then all the ugliness disappears and all the shame is forgotten.

Vronsky: What! This is because of Golenishchev's ineptness which upset you so much.

Anna: No, no. It's something else.

Vronsky: Something else?

Anna: Yes, someone came. A woman who represents to my eyes all that is light, frivolous and low—a woman who has had first one lover, then another, then still others at the taste of her caprice and immorality —and— she treated me like an equal—and she proved to me in the eyes of the world that I am worse than she is—less respectable even, since I abandoned my son and my husband for you, while she is a widow and free, and she has always been able to follow her caprices without injuring anyone!

Vronsky: Anna, who was it?

Anna: What does her name matter? She told me the truth! That's why I ask you, my love, my dear, to love me with all your strength—to the point where I cannot think of anything but our love. I ask you to leave here, to flee from everything that recalls our past so that we can be in a new country and be reborn.

Vronsky: We will leave tomorrow for Naples. Then we will go further still. True liberty is in our hearts and we know the truth in our hearts—since we love each other.

Anna: (in Vronsky's arms) Ah! Yes, yes, yes. Speak to me of this. Reassure me, carry me off. I will close my eyes and I will still see you—and I will forget, I will forget. There's only one reality which—may be a dream.

Vronsky: I love you.

Voices of Some Gondoliers: (in the distance) Ho! Hi! Ho! Ah! Ah! Ah! Ah! Ho! Hi! Ho!

Vladimir: (entering) My Captain. My Captain.

Vronsky: It's you, Vladimir? What's wrong? Why are you so happy?

Vladimir: A visitor! My Captain! The General, His Excellency is here—I am going to bring him.

Vronsky: Who? What Excellency? Speak clearly.

Vladimir: The General Count Serpukhovskoy. He's here to see you.

Vronsky: Well, let him in, let him in.

(Vladimir leaves.)

Anna: I will leave you, my dear.

Vronsky: I am so happy to see him.

Anna: Don't be quite so happy. I am jealous.

Vronsky: Jealous! Of a General!

Anna: Soon!

(Anna goes out at the rear. Vronsky goes joyously towards the door and the right.)

Vronsky: (calling) Serpukhovskoy!

Serpukhovskoy: (entering, followed by Vladimir) Vronsky, my dear Vronsky!

(Vronsky and Serpukhovskoy embrace with great emotion.)

Vronsky: General!

Serpukhovskoy: Quiet down! No General here! It's over three years since we were Captains together—it's twenty years since we were comrades in college. Ah! You are looking fine!

Vronsky: You, too!

Serpukhovskoy: Me? Exhausted, crushed, but solid enough. I have three months leave. I came to spend them in the sun. After two years in Siberia and military tumult—it's nothing to turn your back on.

Vronsky: You are the hero of the day. The papers are full of the noise of your exploits.

Serpukhovskoy: Oh, it's boring enough!

Vronsky: Come on! I know you're ambitious and you've proven you were right to be so. Glory is nothing to fear. Will you have something? Yes? Good. Vladimir. Some champagne, two glasses.

Vladimir: Yes, Captain.

(Vladimir remains in contemplation before Serpukhovskoy.)

Vronsky: Well, stupid! Yes! He's not in uniform, but he's a General all the same. Go! Trot!

(Vladimir tears himself away from the sight of Serpukhovskoy.)

Serpukhovskoy: You took him away?

Vronsky: I got two years leave for him. He is very devoted to me, but he misses the regiment.

Serpukhovskoy: You are nicely set up here.

Vronsky: Yes, it's picturesque.

Serpukhovskoy: And you have a romantic allure which almost makes one forget you were a soldier.

Vronsky: It's the influence of the country.

(Vladimir returns.)

Vronsky: Put that here on the table. Thank you.

Serpukhovskoy: Wait. I am going to uncork it. You know that I excel at this type of sport. We hopped around enough in the private corners of Saint Petersburg when we were lieutenants together. Hoopla!

Vronsky: To your health, brother!

Serpukhovskoy: To your health, brother!

Vronsky: To Russia, as before.

Serpukhovskoy: To Russia.

(Vronsky and Serpukhovskoy kiss on the mouth in the Russian way and drink.)

Vronsky: To your glory!

Serpukhovskoy: To your loves!

Vladimir: And to our father, the Emperor.

Serpukhovskoy: You are still here, straggler?

Vronsky: Why didn't you leave us?

Vladimir: I have something to ask of you, my Captain.

Vronsky: What? What is it?

Vladimir: I want to return to Russia with the General.

Vronsky: You are unhappy in my service?

Vladimir: Oh, no, Captain. But—I'd like to have my horse back. Here one cannot ride. Water is everywhere.

Vronsky: You want to desert? Savage!

(Vronsky kicks out at Vladimir.)

Vladimir: (laughing) That's all right with me, Captain. You know what I think.

(Vladimir leaves.)

Vronsky: And now, let's talk! Wait—smoke!

Serpukhovskoy: As you like.

Vronsky: I have nothing to tell. I am a happy man.

Serpukhovskoy: I know. I have always known what concerned you through my wife. I am glad that you continued to see her often while you were in Saint Petersburg.

Vronsky: She's a friend of Betsy—and the only woman at Saint Petersburg I had the pleasure to see.

Serpukhovskoy: Not absolutely the only one.

Vronsky: Without doubt, without doubt! I wouldn't be here otherwise. And on my side, I have not lost you from sight. I have been very happy over your success. It did not surprise me. I expect even better yet!

Serpukhovskoy: Well, I—I don't hope for any more, I assure you in all frankness. It is true that I am happy. I am ambitious, it's a weakness, without doubt, but I don't hide it.

Vronsky: You will hide it even less if you succeed.

Serpukhovskoy: Perhaps! Besides, my opinion is formal on this subject—and I can open my heart to you, a friend always. I feel myself that it isn't logical that my joy grows and also my will to conquer. I reproach myself every day for being ambitious!

Vronsky: There was a time, friend, not long ago, when I had some opinions on the subject, but at present—

Serpukhovskoy: You still have: like a fire smoldering under ashes.

Vronsky: No, I assure you! I live without ambition, or at least with the sole ambition of protecting my happiness.

Serpukhovskoy: Ah! Ah! There we are!

Vronsky: What do you mean to say?

Serpukhovskoy: Nothing! You permit me to speak frankly? Are we alone?

Vronsky: Of course.

Serpukhovskoy: You won't misconstrue my intentions?

Vronsky: Not for a minute.

Serpukhovskoy: Then, I'll let myself go. I'm not going to play diplomat with you. I reserve such attitudes for my enemies. You refused a mission in Central Asia?

Vronsky: Yes.

Serpukhovskoy: You were free to do so—but you were wrong in my opinion. But, why did you send your resignation to the Emperor? From love?

Vronsky: Yes.

Serpukhovskoy: What a stupidity. My poor Alexei, couldn't you have asked for a leave? A long leave? What the devil! You are enough, you were enough, in Court to obtain a year's leave, if you wished it. You see the country, you have some feeling for it, and you tire of it.

Vronsky: Shut up! It's true I resigned abruptly, and in a kind of madness—but I regret nothing. Ah, God, no! You yourself agree that I was free not to go to Central Asia—Tashkent. My mother would have died of it and, you know, also, the one you I could not, and must not, abandon. These are profound human reasons which they cannot comprehend at Court. They made a bad face. They made life difficult. I didn't like their manner of giving me a lesson in courage.

Serpukhovskoy: Oh, it wasn't anybody's intention—

Vronsky: Yes! Yes! I tell you plainly. They believed that I was inferior to my reputation as a good officer. I surrendered my saber—and that was that!

Serpukhovskoy: If it is true they misjudged you at that time, it is no less true that they regret you today, deeply!

Vronsky: Really?

Serpukhovskoy: Yes, yes! All—from your soldiers who adore you—to your comrades. Yavshine has grown thin. He doesn't drink equal to his thirst except once a week. But I must tell you, his thirst is great.

Vronsky: Oh! The great Yavshine. What a fine boy! And Kouslov, the major?

Serpukhovskoy: He repeats ceaselessly: "There isn't a cavalier left in the regiment since Vronsky left."

Vronsky: And our old fogy of a Colonel Gritzby?

Serpukhovskoy: He cries quite openly when they speak of you.

Vronsky: (moved) The good old brute.

Serpukhovskoy: And that isn't all. I have tested the water—and very diplomatically with the Minister, on the possible re-integration of an officer of your worth.

Vronsky: Why did you do that? Who put you up to it?

Serpukhovskoy: Only my friendship—and my conviction that officers like you are needed.

Vronsky: By whom?

Serpukhovskoy: By whom? By society! By Russia! Russia needs men. She needs protectors. You haven't already gone to seed, have you?

Vronsky: One would have to be blind—

Serpukhovskoy: There needs to be, near the Emperor, a group of powerful men—independent men—who will enlighten him—who will aid him to direct his people, who can teach him how to make himself loved—and who can show him how. It's necessary for us to light the way. But, it's also necessary to pitilessly root out this rabble of lying functionaries, officers of the antechamber, anchored in their privileges, lying to all, to God, to the Emperor, to the people! As dull in their base luxuries as the worst of our mouzhiks in his crassness and ignorance! Vronsky! The Russian people need enlightened leaders and liberty!

Vronsky: You're right. I have often thought this way. But, I no longer belong. Nevertheless, I thank you for having judged me worthy to help you in this task.

Serpukhovskoy: You belong even more now, Alexei, but this won't always last.

Vronsky: That may be—but—

Serpukhovskoy: You said: "That may be." Me, I say, certainly not. Don't say any more about it. I am sure, at present, of not having come in vain, and I know that when I say to you: "Vronsky, I need you" that you will come to your senses.

(Vronsky does not reply.)

Serpukhovskoy: Well, I came to tell you today. Vronsky, return with me to Russia. I have need of you.

Vronsky: I ask for nothing, friend, except that the present continue.

Serpukhovskoy: Listen to me. We are the same age. Perhaps you have known more women than I have, but I am married, and as someone said, a man who knows his wife and loves her, knows more about women than someone who has known a thousand.

Vronsky: Why do you say this to me?

Serpukhovskoy: Women, in my opinion, are the stumbling block in a man's career. When one loves, you see, it is difficult to do good. At least to be married, with the one love—in this case, the only love—does not condemn you to inaction. As far as explaining this to you, admit you carry a weight on your shoulders. Your hands are of no use to you so long as the weight remains there. That's what I found out when I married. My hands became suddenly free. But to drag this weight around without marriage condemns you to inaction. Look at our comrades Mazoupof and Kroupof. Thanks to women, they lost their careers.

Vronsky: But, what women? Third rate actresses, French whores.

Serpukhovskoy: Yes, I agree with you. Nonetheless,

those weights are easier to get rid of. One can be brutal. But, with a woman of high rank, who has failed to attach herself to someone—

Vronsky: You have never loved.

Serpukhovskoy: Perhaps, Alexei, but don't forget this. We have a grandiose idea of love, whereas women always remain down to earth.

(After several seconds Anna enters, without being seen by Serpukhovskoy and Vronsky. She has listened with a growing emotion to this diatribe by Serpukhovskoy which she now interrupts with a scathing voice.)

Anna: You are deceived, Monsieur, women know how to love.

Vronsky: Anna!

Serpukhovskoy: Madame!

Anna: Women know how to love better than you—

Vronsky: Anna! You don't understand.

Anna: Yes, I know. I am committing a mad act and a quite improper one. You have not presented me to General Serpukhovskoy. No matter. We understand each other perfectly—and then, we are not exiles, except from the moral law. Listen to me! Let's leave these worldly constraints. In spite of myself I heard your conversation. At least of the end of your conversation. You made amusing comparisons, General. We are, poor women, heavy burdens to those we love—and we remain down to earth in our love! Pretty excuse for your cowardliness and your lassitude. You have, you say, a grandiose conception of love. But we, who have no conception, neither grandiose nor shabby, who love simply with all our instinct, with all our heart, we sacrifice in a minute our repose, our honor, our rank, our sad motherhood—and we go—confidently—towards the heart we have chosen. Never—never, do we have the idea of analyzing or dissecting our sacrifice. We love, we don't reproach. We love, we don't regret. We love, we never cry over the ruins of our motherhood. We love.

Vronsky: Anna! Anna! What have I done to deserve such vehemence on your part?

Anna: You were listening to him, Alexei, and your protests were so weak, so little categorical, that I suddenly became afraid, my dear, my love. I love you so much. I am almost a mad woman thinking of it.

Serpukhovskoy: Pardon me. I am going.

Anna: No. No.

Serpukhovskoy: Yes, Madame. I must go. But not without expressing to you, from the depths of my heart, all the regrets I feel for having provoked this great emotion, these tears.

Anna: I don't wish it. You love him, too. You are only looking out for his good.

Serpukhovskoy: I have faith in him, it's true.

Anna: Then, take my hand, General. I believe we shall know each other better.

Serpukhovskoy: Madame.

Anna: Rest easy. I know how to love him.

Serpukhovskoy: I am sure of it.

Anna: Yes, yes, I know how.

Serpukhovskoy: Adieu, Vronsky.

Vronsky: Adieu, General.

Anna: Not adieu—à bientôt.

(Serpukhovskoy leaves. A long silence.)

Anna: You forgive me, Alexei?

Vronsky: I have nothing to forgive you. I love you.

Anna: I thank heaven for sending me the strength to see things as they are in their true colors.

Vronsky: What do you mean?

Anna: We've got to leave.

Vronsky: We will leave tomorrow.

Anna: (interrupting him) For Russia. For Saint Petersburg! You must resume your work, so you can be ambitious. I must get my husband to consent to a divorce, so that I may be your wife before everyone, so that your hands may be free. This weight—do you accept it with joy, Alexei?

Vronsky: My dearly loved one!

Anna: Then, let's go. Let's leave immediately. We weren't made for this existence on the margin. We didn't count on our pride, on our honor which suffers in this errant life of our doubtful relations, on these lies, more vile than those we left behind. We've got to start our true life again! Do you want to?

Vronsky: Your will is my will, Anna.

Anna: Hold me tight—tight—tight. Are you happy with me?

Vronsky: I love you!

CURTAIN

ACT IV

Same as Act II. Karenin's. At rise, Seriozha is seated at his father's desk. Kapitonich, the old Swiss, is seated in front of him. At the right, the tutor, Vassilii Lukich, is seated with his back to the audience. Kapitonich is finishing a story.

Seriozha: And then?

Kapitonich: And then, Excellency— Boom! A great explosion like an earthquake and everything—pell-mell, English, Russians, French. The devil himself could not have seen the color of his soul. I got a sharp knock on the heard and then I didn't think any more.

Seriozha: And then?

Kapitonich: And then—that's how I earned my medal— and there it was—I swear to God and our emperor.

Seriozha: There were dead and wounded?

Kapitonich: Thousands of dead and hundreds wounded!

Vassilii: (joking) I myself will teach history to Seriozha Alexeivitch, old veteran. Return to your post.

Kapitonich: (threatening) Little shrimp! Bad little Russian. Teacher of penmanship.

Seriozha: (laughing) There, there. It's my relaxation. Kapitonich can stay with me. Papa permits him.

Vassilii: If His Excellency Alexei Alexandrovich knew what nonsense this old fool tells you—

Seriozha: Right! You must not listen, Vassilii Lukich! What is your medal, Kapitonich?

Kapitonich: It's the Saint George.

Seriozha: Ah. Is your daughter well?

Kapitonich: Yes, Excellency.

Seriozha: She is happy with her job?

Kapitonich: Oh, yes and no. It's living to jump and turn—one—two—three. And the ballet master, who is French, is terrible. Anyway, that's what she says.

Seriozha: You know how to dance, too?

Kapitonich: I knew.

Seriozha: What? The trepak?

Kapitonich: No, the kazachouk. And I could sing, too.

Seriozha: Then dance the kazachouk for me.

Kapitonich: Truly, Excellency—

Seriozha: Dance. I wish it!

(Kapitonich tries to dance and then lets himself fall slowly.)

Kapitonich: Aie! Aie! Aie! My rheumatism.

Seriozha:
  You cannot dance.

Kapitonich: Not any more. But I can still sing.

Seriozha: Well, then, sing. Sing.

Kapitonich: (with a thunderous voice) There was a little black dog—

Vassilii: Hush! Hush! Enough! Enough!

Seriozha: Oh, oh, bravo! Continue! Continue!

Vassilii: If His Excellency Alexei Alexandrovich hears you—God protect me. What a voice!

Kapitonich: (laughing) Fine, let him shut up then. He's jealous.

Seriozha: That's it. Get down on all fours.

Kapitonich: What, Excellency? Ha! Ha! Ha! On all fours?

Seriozha: You will be the horse and I will be the rider.

Vassilii: In five minutes recess will be over.

Seriozha: Yes, yes, but until then I am the master. The office is mine for now. I can do what I please. Hoopla, gallop! (jumping on Kapitonich's back) Yah! Yah! (to Matrona who enters) Niania! Niania! Look how well your husband gallops.

Matrona: (to Kapitonich) Merciful God! Are you still amusing yourself, you old beast? Rascal, and you sang so loud the windows in the house were shaking. But think, if His Excellency Alexei Alexandrovich came and you were not at your post, at the door below—

Kapitonich: But, my little mother—we must have a little fun. Get down, Monsieur Seriozha.

Seriozha: No, no.

Matrona: Get down, get down. Right away.

Seriozha: Yes, but on one condition. Listen to this, Matrona.

Matrona: What, my God. What, scamp?

Seriozha: You'll talk about Mama again.

Matrona: Yes, yes. That I promise.

Seriozha: Then I'll get down.

Matrona: About time!

Kapitonich: (rising, to Matrona) And what did His Excellency say when he saw I wasn't at my post?

Matrona: He said nothing, old fool, because he hasn't yet returned from the cabinet meeting.

Kapitonich: Good, I will save myself. Good day until tomorrow, Excellency. We will do it again. (pointing to Vassilii) It will be his turn to go on all fours.

(Kapitonich leaves, laughing.)

Vassilii: (furious) Ah, if he wasn't so big and— Two more minutes, Seriozha Alexeivitch.

Seriozha: (to Matrona) You know what you promised me? Have you got a letter, some news? Is she coming to see me soon? Is she still in Moscow?

Matrona: There, there, softly, my little soul. Your mother wrote me. She's fine and she prays God that you will be worthy—

Seriozha: Then she is not dead! That old Lidia Ivanovna told me she was dead. Why did she tell me that?

Matrona: She is lying! Anna Arkadyevna isn't dead, praise Christ!

(Seriozha and Matrona have been speaking in hushed tones. Vassilii steps unexpectedly between them.)

Vassilii: Why do you speak so low? His Excellency forbids it! He wants me to hear everything that people say to Seriozha Alexeivitch.

Matrona: Come, then and listen! You know, indeed, of what I speak and you think like all the old retainers in this house—like Kapitonich—like me.

Vassilii: (hiding his emotion) Leave us! The recess is over.

Matrona: Fine! Fine! Your eyes shine, you are only a little Russian, but you have a good heart. Goodbye, little one.

Seriozha: Goodbye Niania.

(As soon as the old nurse leaves, Vassilii Lukich claps his hands.)

Vassilii: Come! Come! You've got to get to work now, Seriozha Alexeivitch. It is already ten o'clock. You'll never finish your lesson about the history of the saints.

Seriozha: No geography, Vassilii Lukich. What difference does it make?

Vassilii: For goodness sake!

Seriozha: Tomorrow is my birthday. Papa will not have the courage to punish me. Neither will the "living horror."

Vassilii: Monsieur!

Seriozha: Good! That's what I am going to tell her. Countess Lidia Ivanovna—the dirty pig!

Vassilii: Why do you detest her so? She's good to you.

Seriozha: No, she's severe and mean. And then—

Vassilii: And then?

Seriozha: And then, she wishes to make me believe things which are not true.

Vassilii: It is impossible that Lidia, who is a person so pious, told a lie, even the smallest.

Seriozha: She is a liar!

Vassilii: Monsieur!

Seriozha: Yes, we have proof of it, Matrona and I! Why does she tell me that Mama is dead when Matrona, who was Mama's nurse, told me she was alive? Mama is in Moscow, living with Uncle Stiva. I know it, I saw her leave. She kissed me. And, it's true, since you say nothing!

Vassilii: Learn your patriarchs, Monsieur Seriozha. In five minutes, His Excellency will come to test you and you won't know them.

Seriozha: Bah! If I studied, I wouldn't know any more. Papa knows the Old Testament only because he tests me with the book open in front of him. Besides, Papa won't be severe. He received a decoration today so he must be happy.

Vassilii: Why not be happy to receive recognition from the Emperor? Isn't it proof he deserved it?

Seriozha: Yes! This decoration is the Alexander Nevsky, isn't it?

Vassilii: Yes.

Seriozha: What other decorations does he have?

Vassilii: The Vladimir.

Seriozha: And, besides that?

Vassilii: Above all, the Saint Andrew.

Seriozha: When I grow up, I intend to have all the medals.

Vassilii: You must work hard to deserve them.

Seriozha: I will.

Vassilii: Your lesson, then, Seriozha Alexeivitch.

Seriozha: Yes, yes. Listen, Vassilii Lukich, yesterday, in the summer garden, I saw a beautiful, oh, so beautiful lady with a blue veil. I thought it was Mama. I looked at her with such a desire to kiss her and say to her: "I am your little Seriozha, Mama." She wasn't there when I went back; instead, the living horror was there.

Vassilii: You are a bad boy, Monsieur.

Seriozha: Me, oh?

Vassilii: Here's His Excellency.

(Alexei Karenin enters. Seriozha runs to him and kisses him.)

Seriozha: Bonjour, Papa.

Karenin: Bonjour, Seriozha. Bonjour, Vassilii Lukich.

Vassilii: Excellency.

Karenin: You can leave us, Vassilii Lukich. Seriozha studied hard? He wasn't too restless?

Vassilii: He has been very peaceful, Excellency.

Karenin: Fine.

(Vassilii leaves.)

Karenin: Did you take a nice walk yesterday? I haven't seen you because I was dining with the minister at his home.

Seriozha: Yes, Papa, very nice. I am much amused with Nadinka in the summer garden. Nadinka told me that you received another medal. Are you happy with it, Papa?

Karenin: First of all, don't calculate like that. I've told you twenty times. As to the medal, remember that only the work can make you happy, not its reward. Truly, one has to work. Work will seem useless if you want only the reward, while, if you love your work, you will always have your reward. Do you understand?

Seriozha: Yes, Papa.

Karenin: Good. Now, tell me your lesson. Let's see. The Patriarchs. Who where they?

Seriozha: First of all Enoch.

Karenin: No, not the first. Still, Enoch. Who was Enoch?

Seriozha: He was Methuselah's father.

Karenin: Good. Who was Methuselah?

Seriozha: He was an old man.

Karenin: What are you saying?

Seriozha: He was an old man who didn't want to die. He was right, Papa. Do you believe in death?

Karenin: What a singular question!

Seriozha: Me, I don't believe in death. For example, I don't believe that Mama is dead. And you, Papa?

Karenin: One doesn't discuss such questions with a child of your age. The Patriarchs?

Seriozha: Enoch, father of Methuselah—Enoch.

Karenin: Is that all you know?

Seriozha: Yes, Papa.

Karenin: That's bad, Seriozha. That's bad. If you don't take care of instructing yourself with things essential for a Christian to know, then what will you occupy yourself with? I am going to be obliged to punish you. You will lunch alone here this morning.

Seriozha: All right, Papa.

(Vassilii enters.)

Karenin: What is it, Vassilii Lukich?

Vassilii: The Countess Lidia Ivanovna would like—

Karenin: Come in, come in, dear friend.

(Lidia Ivanovna enters.)

Karenin: You are none too soon. (pointing to Seriozha) He is lazy. I am very unhappy with him.

Lidia: I would like to speak with you alone, Alexei Alexandrovich.

Karenin: All right. Vassilii, go to the greenhouse with Seriozha. I will call you back later.

Vassilii: Fine, Excellency.

Seriozha: I'm happy, Vassilii. I am punished.

Vassilii: And that makes you happy?

Seriozha: I won't have to eat lunch looking that old hag in the face. Pouah! She ruins my appetite.

Vassilii: Oh, Monsieur, Monsieur.

(Vassilii and Seriozha leave.)

Karenin: I am not happy with Seriozha. I find in him a certain coldness toward the essential questions that ought to touch the human heart, even in a child.

Lidia: But his heart—I find in him the heart of his father, and with that, can he be bad? Anyway, that's not the question. May the merciful God give you, in these circumstances, my friend, the strength of soul that he has so often lavished on you many times before. They are in Saint Petersburg—those villainous people have returned!

Karenin: Oh!

Lidia: I can't imagine they will dare to stay here for long. They will soon take up their adventurous ways again. But now, at the moment, they are here. Here's the letter that Anna Arkadyevna had the nerve to write me.

(Lidia offers Karenin a paper.)

Karenin: (very upset) You read it. The words dance before my eyes. This writing recalls to me so many painful memories.

Lidia: Courage! (reading) "Countess, you are a fervent Christian. You will pardon my writing, but for some time I have not seen my son. Understand the anguish of my heart and permit me to see him once, alone, wherever you wish, whenever you wish. Be my advocate with Alexei Alexandrovich. I dare not address him directly. I have caused him enough sorrow already. You won't refuse me this maternal kiss. You will accept my sincere thanks. Anna."

Karenin: How long have you had this letter?

Lidia: Since yesterday, during the ceremony for your medal. Christ imposes his cross on you, but he gives you the strength to bear it.

Karenin: I don't believe I have the right to refuse her.

Lidia: My friend, you don't want to see the evil here—

Karenin: But, yes, yes, to the contrary. If you knew what a pessimist and skeptic I am. Is it possible—is it just to refuse her?

Lidia: No, no. There are limits to everything. I understand immorality, but I don't understand cruelty towards a man like you. Why does she come to Saint Petersburg to expose you to the chance of meeting her? What baseness.

Karenin: But, since you know the depths of my heart, since it was you who reawakened in me the Christian beliefs which allowed me to forgive them—to judge that their punishment was in their own hands—in the false situation they have created—have I the right to thwart her maternal love?

Lidia: Seriozha believes she is dead! Each day I have him pray for her—for the pardon of her sins. If he were to see her, what trouble would this cause the young innocent child? What questions would he ask you, which, if they remain unanswered, must debase a sacred memory?

Karenin: You are right. I didn't think of that.

Lidia: But I thought of it! Guided by The One who gives us the courage to submit to our fate without rebelling.

Karenin: You are my second conscience.

Lidia: Anna must understand that to see her child is a criminal thing. Hasn't she done you enough evil already? And while the occasion serves, I ought to mention something I have observed—this scandal has done you no credit.

Karenin: I don't find that to be true, Lidia Ivanovna. I am still listened to, God be thanked, at the Imperial Council and the Emperor has given me proof of his satisfaction, but still—

Lidia: Yes, the decoration! But you know very well the governmental procedures to ignore the meaning of your decoration. When a man who has occupied a very high position is finished, they cover him with honorary titles. They disarm him completely with a bauble. A month after Vronsky and your wife left, you were no longer Minister. You won't regain that position soon—and it is because of ridicule—here, like everywhere, which puts you in the wrong!

Karenin: You are right. We must refuse this interview.

Lidia: You know the depths of your heart. I will reply to this woman as soon as possible that you refuse to let her see Seriozha.

Karenin: Thank you. I might not have had the courage.

Lidia: Say: the necessary clear-sightedness.

Karenin: Your vigilance gives me such a moral repose. Will you accept my arm, Lidia Ivanovna? I believe it is time to think of lunch.

Lidia: I'm happy to carry out your ideas concerning this letter.

(Exit Karenin and Lidia. The stage is empty. A long pause. Kapitonich reenters. He goes to the door by which Lidia and Karenin left, listens, then retraces his steps to the door by which he entered, murmuring.)

Kapitonich: Good! It's just as I hoped. They are at lunch.

(Popoff, the coachman, enters. Anna is behind him in the doorway.)

Kapitonich: (to Popoff) Close your eyes. (to Anna) This way, Excellency. Here is the new study hall of Seriozha Alexeivitch. Excuse, if all is in disorder.

Anna: Merci, Kapitonich, merci. Go find him quickly. Please find him.

Kapitonich: He won't be too far away. His preceptor, Vassilii Lukich, told me that he was being punished and had to eat lunch alone, here in his room. Oh, don't worry. His Excellency Alexei Alexandrovich is having his lunch now.

Seriozha: (entering, aside low) Kapitonich told me a lady! Good, as long as it is not the living horror. I was afraid— (aloud) Bonjour, Madame.

(Anna rises excitedly, goes to her son and takes him in her arms. She is holding him; he can't say a word. Seriozha disengages himself, then looks at his mother and hurls himself back into her arms.)

Seriozha: Mama!

Anna: (embracing him almost to the point of suffocation) Seriozha! Seriozha! My little Seriozha!

Seriozha: I knew very well that you were coming. I knew you weren't dead, my pretty Mama.

Anna: How handsome you are! How you have grown!

Seriozha: Why are you crying, Mama? Tell me why you are crying.

Anna: Me? But, I am not crying. It's the joy of seeing

you. It's been such a long time since I last saw you. Now it's over.

Seriozha: How happy I am to be punished today.

Anna: You are being punished?

Seriozha: Yes. I have to eat here all alone. So much the worse—you don't get to see the dining room. (kissing her) They told me you were dead, but—I didn't believe them. I knew you were in Moscow with Uncle Stiva! Did you bring something for me?

Anna: Oh, lord—toys! I was in such a hurry to see you, my dear. I left them in the carriage.

Seriozha: That won't matter, Mama. Vassilii will go to get them later. Ah, here's Vassilii. Look, Mama's come back. Why are you crying too, Vassilii?

Vassilii: Excellency!

Anna: Bonjour, Vassilii Lukich. Don't worry, I'm going to leave. Five minutes. Just give me five minutes with him.

Vassilii: Just five minutes, then, Excellency.

Seriozha: Mama! Grisha and Tania and Vasya come sometimes. You know, it's sad here since you left.

Anna: Ah!

Seriozha: Yes! And Papa is so strict about my lessons. He's teaching me the history of the Saints at present. Each time that I asked him where you were, he only looked more sad. Then, there is that old living horror.

Anna: Who?

Seriozha: Lidia Ivanovna. I detest her.

Anna: Is she mean to you?

Seriozha: No. Sweet, sweet. Pouah! Too sweet. She's a liar! Why did she tell me that you were dead? She is boring, too, you know.

(Old Matrona enters and listens, without moving.)

Seriozha: The house is not gay because of that dirty old pig. Let's go. In the summer garden we can play. There we can do what we want.

Matrona: Madame! My love! Here's a joy sent by God to Seriozha Alexeivitch. How pretty you are, my dove! More beautiful than ever.

Seriozha: Mama, she always told me you'd come to see me.

Anna: Oh, hold me, hold me truly, Nurse, if you still love me.

Matrona: Nothing in this world will stop me from loving you.

Anna: Niania, my dear! You must tell me something. (low to Seriozha) Leave me a minute, dear. (to Matrona) Does Lidia Ivanovna come here often?

Matrona: Yes.

Anna: Is she the mistress of my husband?

Matrona: Who told you that, my dove?

Anna: Everyone is saying so!

Matrona: And everyone is lying.

Anna: But, no! Don't hide anything from me, Niania, if you love me. Maybe, it must—let it be, so he can feel some guilt himself—so he will agree to a divorce.

Matrona: (firmly) There's no truth in what they say about them!

Anna: You swear to me on the Saints?

Matrona: I swear to you, your husband is irreproachable.

Anna: Then all is lost, now. If he isn't guilty, I have no argument against him. He will agree to nothing. He's right! He's right!

Kapitonich: (entering) Excellency. The valet de chambre to Alexei Alexandrovich has informed His Excellency that you are here.

Anna: Oh, my God! My God!

(Anna prepares to leave.)

Seriozha: Don't go yet, Mama. He won't come so soon.

Anna: My dear! My little dear! You won't ever forget your mother? Take him away, Matrona. Love your father, my treasure, love him well. He is better than I am.

When you grow up, you will judge. I've been guilty towards him.

Seriozha: No one is better than you!

Anna: My little soul! My dear!

Kapitonich: His Excellency is coming!

Anna: Take him! Take him, Matrona, quickly.

Seriozha: Mama!

Anna: Adieu!

(Karenin enters. He is very pale and holds himself motionless and glacial. Anna tries to speak.)

Anna: Alexei, I thought— My son! Pardon!

(Karenin just points to the open door. Anna, without a word, lowers her veil and leaves, shaking with tears.)

CURTAIN

ACT V

The terrace of a country house on the outskirts of Moscow. In the rear, a panorama of the Holy City. At rise, Vladimir is alone on the stage. We can hear Annoushka's voice.

Annoushka: Vladimir! Vladimir!

Vladimir: Is that you, Annoushka?

Annoushka: Yes. There are visitors from Moscow for Colonel Vronsky and Anna Arkadyevna. Should I bring them here to the terrace or would it be better in the house?

Vladimir: Wherever you wish, little mother. It's all the same to me.

Annoushka: I believe it is the brother of Anna Arkadyevna and his wife. Holy archangels! Let it not be bad news for Count Vronsky.

Vladimir: Why's that, Annoushka?

Annoushka: Alas! The devil is so mean! Everything that concerns the Barinia does not inspire me with confidence, you know. The priest told me she is living in a state of perpetual sin.

Vladimir: The priest is an imbecile! Isn't she good to you and everyone?

Annoushka: Angels in heaven. How brutal you are since he became Colonel. Can't one talk? One cannot say anything about her! You would deny she's living in concubinage—that she's an adulterous spouse! And if I was Count Vronsky, what wouldn't I be thinking?

Vladimir: Enough gossip! Bad beast! Old hag!

Annoushka: Ah, men. You are all on her side because she's pretty.

(Enter Stiva and Dolly.)

Stiva: Well, you forgot us in the park. Have you told Anna Arkadyevna of our visit?

Annoushka: Not yet, little uncle. I was asking Vladimir if the Barinia was there.

(Annoushka goes into the house which overlooks a railway track leading to Moscow.)

Stiva: In that case get going. (to Dolly) The evenings are cold this time of year. I hope we can return to Moscow before evening. We have a good half hour by carriage.

Dolly: Perhaps Anna will want to keep us to dinner.

Stiva: Don't think of it! My official character—we must not lose sight for even a minute of Anna's moral situation. I love her deeply, but our family relations will only be publicly reestablished when the day arrives that she is divorced and becomes Countess Vronsky.

Dolly: It seems to me, Stiva, that you should have more understanding and less concern for public opinion.

Stiva: Pardon me. I came here as Alexei Alexandrovich's representative and not as Anna's brother.

Dolly: You ought to conciliate matters.

Stiva: Duty must come before feelings.

Annoushka: (entering) Anna Arkadyevna begs you to wait for her here. She is coming right away. Peter! And you, Nicolas! Haven't I told you a hundred times!

Stiva: What is going on?

Annoushka: It's my naughty boy, Excellency, and my nephew Nicolas. They help in the kitchen and they are both villainous devils. (to Peter) I'll make you eat with that scamp, Damavoi!

(Peter and Nicolas enter. Nicolas is ready to cry. He has two live chickens which he is holding by their feet.)

Stiva: Where are these scamps coming from?

Annoushka: They're coming from Vassilii Mikaloff's, the Mouzhik, to get chickens for dinner. And so as not to take a long detour around the railway bridge. They crossed the tracks. (to Peter and Nicolas) And if Count Vronsky had seen you?

(Peter laughs and makes a negative motion.)

Annoushka: Peter, you lead Nicolas into trouble. Vassilii traps in the woods to catch rabbits. He will catch you one day.

Peter: No.

Annoushka: Go in, you devils. (she hustles them away) And that's for you, Peter. (gives him a slap) If I catch you going there again, watch out.

Peter: You won't catch us.

(The children and Annoushka go out.)

Stiva: I hadn't noticed this little stairway.

Vladimir: It's a passage for the VIPs who know the train schedules. The Count uses it to better watch his hunting grounds. You can see a long way from there.

Stiva: It would be very dangerous for children if the door is left open.

Dolly: It would be firmly shut, without doubt, if Seriozha were living with his mother.

(Stiva goes to the balustrade in the rear and looks at the view.)

Stiva: Doubtless this area near the railway line would be very disagreeable. Is it the Nijni line?

Vladimir: Yes, Excellency. It passes through Obiralovka where Colonel Vronsky goes to see his mother. When he goes there two or three times a week, it passes under Anna Arkadyevna's window and they can see each other.

Stiva: (looking at Vladimir for a moment) Where have I seen you before?

Vladimir: At Tsarkoe Selo, Excellency, at the races three years ago. Oh, I recognized you quite easily.

Stiva: But you didn't have this on your shoulder.

Vladimir: Oh, that! General Minister Serpukhovskoy had it given to me about six months after Count Vronsky became a Colonel.

(While this colloquy is taking place in the center of the stage, Dolly goes toward the house and Anna comes out.)

Dolly: My dear, Anna. My dear, Anna, how happy I am to see you.

Anna: Dolly, my Dolly.

(Anna and Dolly embrace a long while with great emotion. Stiva leaves Vladimir and approaches Anna. Vladimir exits.)

Stiva: I embrace you very willingly, also, my dear sister.

Anna: Oh, Stiva, Stiva, it's such a long time since I saw you last. And so very many things have happened since then. Just now, when they told me you were here, I was almost sick with joy. Thank you Stiva! Thank you, my dear Dolly!

Dolly: You've had some rough times to endure, dear Anna, but we all have times in our lives which appear so dark that it seems we'll never find the light. Time softens all suffering.

Anna: Time doesn't correct irreparable errors. No, my dear Dolly, don't try to console me. I am clairvoyant, very clairvoyant.

Stiva: (very irritated) Hum! Hum! My dear Anna, my dear Anna. It seems that Dolly can tell you better than I the purpose of our visit. If you will allow me, I will go with Vladimir to meet Vronsky. Where is he, exactly?

Anna: He's riding with Captain Makhotin. Our cousin, Princess Barbe Oblonsky, is following them in a carriage.

Stiva: You receive that old infatuated fool, Barbe?

Anna: (with bitterness) I have no choice in relations, but then I mustn't be choosy.

Stiva: I'm not saying this to anger you, but she has a reputation!

Anna: (a little sadly) But, I, too, have a reputation, Stiva.

Dolly: Anna!

Anna: It doesn't matter, Dolly. He didn't mean that exactly.

Stiva: (calling) Vladimir! Vladimir! Which way did your Colonel go?

Vladimir: (replying from off stage) Towards Moscow, Excellency—over here—on this side. I will show you.

(Exit Stiva. Stiva's and Vladimir's voices fade. Anna and Dolly sit on a stone bench.)

Anna: Why did you come, Dolly?

Dolly: We came, Stiva and I, on behalf of your husband.

Anna: On behalf of— Oh! My son is sick! There is something, an illness, a catastrophe which they are hiding from me. Tell me, tell me!

Dolly: But, no, my dear. Seriozha is well, very well.

Anna: You're not lying?

Dolly: Why would I lie?

Anna: At first I was afraid to see you. So moved by both of you. Understand me, Dolly. You are a mother. You have beautiful children that you keep in your arms. You have their first smile in the morning, their kiss in the evening, their lessons, the shared meals, and all the endless worries of maternity. I—I have nothing of my son—except pictures and letters written stealthily which, alas, Matrona sends me so rarely. Perhaps he will forget me. They speak to him of his mother with scorn. Since I left my husband more than two years ago, I have seen him only once for five minutes. They tore him from my arms. I was like a thief in my own house.

Dolly: Be calm, Anna.

Anna: When I think that I can never reunite the two people that I love in this world— Seriozha and Vronsky. Never, never.

Dolly: Yes, Anna! You can, soon perhaps.

Anna: What are you saying? It's impossible.

Dolly: No, Anna. Once married to Vronsky nothing will prevent you from seeing your son. And that is exactly the purpose of our visit. Your husband consents to a divorce.

(There is a long pause. Anna says nothing.)

Dolly: I hoped that would make you happy—and you are so quiet.

Anna: It's too late.

Dolly: How can you say such a thing?

Anna: Two years ago, a year ago, perhaps, I would have been happy—so happy about this news—but today I am the mistress of Colonel Vronsky and only that. He will never allow me to become his wife.

Dolly: You judge him wrongly, Anna.

Anna: He's a man, Dolly! I've made every sacrifice for him. Every sacrifice. But that isn't what he won't forget. It's my modesty.

Dolly: Anna, Anna! You deceive yourself. Your situation is causing a misunderstanding between you. But, think of the children that may be born of your love. They need a father. They don't want to blush for you.

Anna: (violently) I won't have any more children.

Dolly: How can you say that?

Anna: I won't have any more. I shouldn't be a mother, do you understand? I am his mistress. Ah, Dolly, I have so much trouble to keep him already. He knows so well how to find excuses to get away from me. With what enthusiasm has he become a soldier again. If you knew. I am an irritant in his life. He leaves me alone here for weeks and months. I live from day to day—scorned by all—scorned by myself.

Dolly: I don't scorn you, Anna. I have never scorned you.

Anna: You are good! But the others, those whom I hurt, my husband, Kitty, my pretty Kitty.

Dolly: Kitty has pardoned you. She is very happy. She has married Levin. She owes her happiness to you. Sit down again, Anna. Accept the divorce so you may marry the man who loves you and whom you love.

Anna: He doesn't love me any more.

Dolly: Anna, you are unjust! He wanted to die for you. He sacrificed everything for you. His life.

Anna: His life! His life is more brilliant than ever. He's begun it over far from me—and each day pushes him further away! Little by little this great love which ought to ennoble our existence has become a thing that's low and repulsive, an ignominious habit. The end is complete now. I am surrounded by people of ill repute; I was publicly insulted at the Opera in Saint Petersburg like a low woman. There's nothing worse to come.

Dolly: His duty is to marry you when you are free.

Anna: Don't speak to me of duty. That word horrifies me! Where was my duty when I abandoned my son and my husband?

Dolly: Then, I will have come in vain.

Anna: No—since I've cried for you and now I've seen you. Who can tell when I'll see you again?

Dolly: (frightened) Anna!

Anna: He doesn't love me anymore, but I love him—and I have him often near me. You see how demanding I've become. But, from the day I am certain that he loves another woman, my duty will be to set him free. He will be free.

Dolly: (frightened by the resolution she sees in Anna's expression) Anna, my dear. Someone told you—someone told you something.

Anna: (suddenly tragic) And you—you know something?

Dolly: Me? I know something? What are you saying?

Anna: They told you that Countess Vronsky wants to marry her son with the daughter of Princess Sarokine. Don't lie.

Dolly: I swear to you, Anna—

Anna: Don't lie! It's useless! Besides, you owe me the truth. Don't worry about hurting me. I'm used to it.

Dolly: (hurt) They told me—in fact—sometimes there's a slander of this type.

Anna: You see quite well—

Dolly: But, the scandal comes from below—from the

Princess Miaghkaia—to tell you everything.

Anna: She has good reason to hate me!

Dolly: I answered that Vronsky was, above everything, a man of honor and, in the meantime, your husband, on a governmental mission to Moscow, having paid us a visit, Stiva and I obtained his consent to your divorce. We ran here, full of happiness to bring you certainty, that within six months you will be able to become the wife of the man you love and who loves you.

Anna: Oh! If he still loved me! With what joy I would greet this news.

Dolly: Stiva is putting him in the picture right now; he will come back so happy, I am sure of it.

Anna: If he loves me—with what vehemence he will force me to accept the divorce!

Dolly: (smiling) He will do you this violence, Anna, my dear, Anna.

Anna: I wish I could partake of your confidence. Alas, look!

(Stiva and Vronsky appear in the distance. Vronsky is preoccupied and silent.)

Dolly: Madwoman! He doesn't know yet.

Anna: He knows!

(Vronsky kisses the hand of Dolly, then goes to hug Anna.)

Vronsky: (to Dolly) I'm happy to greet you here, Darya Alexandrovna!

Dolly: I, too, Alexei Vronsky.

Anna: (to Vronsky) You come back alone?

Vronsky: Princess Barbe and Makhotin went around the woods. They will be here any minute.

Stiva: Yes. I met Vronsky alone a hundred meters from the gate. Now we should leave.

Anna: What! Won't you dine with us?

Stiva: No, my dear Anna. It's impossible. We have an official dinner tonight —my colleagues of the Court.

Anna: Then, let Dolly stay. Vronsky will take her back.

Vronsky: You know I'm dining with my mother tonight, Anna.

Anna: Ah, yes, yes. I had forgotten.

Dolly: In any event, I wouldn't have abandoned my husband, Alexei. Besides, this first visit doesn't count. Anna, we will return. (to Vronsky) Anna will tell you why we came today.

Stiva: I have already told him, just now.

Dolly: (to Vronsky) You know?

Vronsky: I know.

Dolly: And, have you considered the reply we must take back?

Vronsky: But, it seems to me that the decision doesn't depend on me alone.

Dolly: Indeed, the main interest is Anna's?

Vronsky: Isn't it?

Dolly: Nevertheless—

Anna: (with false gaiety) But, why are you worried, Dolly? I've already told you everything on this subject. The only response is this one: we are perfectly happy—our joy is in our own keeping—we desire nothing that would change our way of life. That's right, isn't it, Aloysha?

Dolly: Anna! Anna!

Anna: (very much mistress of herself) It's by your advice, Alexei, that we leave things as they are?

Vronsky: But, yes, let it be as you will, Anna.

(Stiva grabs Vronsky by the arm and pulls him aside, away from Dolly and Anna.)

Stiva: Think also of what I told you, Vronsky. Serpukhovskoy is all—powerful— (they come back) If he wants to give me a little pat on the shoulder, it's a fifty thousand ruble blessing!

Anna: You see. Everything is finished, indeed!

Dolly: Anna, don't worry yourself like this. You frighten me.

Anna: Adieu, Dolly. Hug your children for me—hug them—hug them—you are happy.

Stiva: Come on, come on. Enough of these affectionate demonstrations. We are in a rush, little sister. Soon—good health—good hopes.

Anna: Adieu, Stiva.

Vronsky: I will accompany you to your carriage.

(They leave. Anna stays motionless. The wind rises. The day starts to end.)

Anna: The night—already night—where is the Venetian sun?

(Vronsky comes back. He stands near Anna.)

Vronsky: I must hug you, too, my dear. I must leave in nearly an hour for the Nijni station.

Anna: Where are you going?

Vronsky: To rejoin General Serpukhovskoy, with whom we must pass the evening at my mother's house.

Anna: Don't go out this evening. Don't go.

Vronsky: Why this caprice, Anna? I promised them I would go.

Anna: Listen, I need to see you, to be with you, to discuss the propositions that were made just now.

Vronsky: Haven't you decided already? You know very well that my will is yours. Whatever you decided, my duty is to obey you.

Anna: (furiously) Duty! Always duty! With that word—and two or three others—conscience, honor—all baseness is masked.

Vronsky: Why this violence, Anna?

Anna: Because I am very nervous and I am very afraid.

Vronsky: You are afraid?

Anna: Yes, you know—you know I'm like a child. I'm afraid to be alone this evening.

Vronsky: A night is quickly over. I will be back tomorrow at ten o'clock.

Anna: Listen. I had my horrible dream yesterday. The one which always tells me of misfortune. I've seen the little dirty old Mouzhik who does invisible things in a sack. I've seen him twice already.

Vronsky: You are not being reasonable, Anna.

Anna: Oh, I know. But, you must treat me gently, like a sick child. I'm afraid of this Mouzhik. You must stay to protect me.

Vronsky: (trying to disengage) I promised, Anna. Let me go!

Anna: (suddenly pushing him away) Well, go then, go! (then holding him again) Where did you tell me you were going?

Vronsky: To meet Serpukhovskoy in Moscow and go to my mother's for a family reunion.

Anna: You swear to me? That's really where you are going?

Vronsky: That's exactly where I am going. As for giving you my word on such a silly subject, and for me not to go and besides, where do you think I am going? Such a demand becomes an insult. I am angry, Anna, that you accuse me of such a wrong.

Anna: Ah, you see my faults now. (trying to smile) And I still don't know any of your faults? Stay Aloysha. Stay this evening. We have a lot to talk about, to say to each other.

Vronsky: I promised. I must leave.

Anna: Are you the slave of your word? Well, you've sworn before to satisfy all my caprices—and since I'm afraid of the little Mouzhik—I insist you stay here.

Vronsky: Impossible.

Anna: Vronsky—

(Princess Barbe and Makhotin enter.)

Vronsky: You are not going to make a scene before them. Goodbye, my dear.

(Vronsky hugs Anna. She remains unmoved. Barbe, who has seen Vronsky embrace Anna, jokes ironically.)

Barbe: Well, well. It's your youth, I know, but you are not in your room here.

Vronsky: A man can hug his wife when he's going on a trip.

Makhotin: You are going to your mother's, Colonel?

Vronsky: Yes, Makhotin. And I confide my wife and the Princess to you.

Barbe: Oh, don't bother to confide me any more. Really, am I a child that needs watching?

Vronsky: You are slandering yourself. Till tomorrow, my dear!

Anna: Till tomorrow.

(Anna watches Vronsky leave and returns to Princess Barbe. On the horizon, Moscow is red under the rays of the setting sun.)

Barbe: You've had some visitors, Anna Arkadyevna?

Anna: Yes. My brother and sister-in-law.

Barbe: They were in a hurry to return to Moscow.

Makhotin: All the world's in a hurry today. There's Vronsky, who's leaving in the caboose at the end of the train. (to Anna) Is it possible he can leave a woman like you in such haste?

(The dinner bell sounds softly.)

Barbe: Dinner? Already? Did they advance the hour today?

Makhotin: No, I believe not. It is, indeed, six-thirty.

Barbe: I'm not angry about it. Besides, our promenade has given me an appetite. Let me go before you. (pointing to Makhotin) Here's another one, dying of love for you, Enchantress.

Anna: Barbe Mikaelovna!

Barbe: All right, all right. I'll shut up. I'll shut up.

(Barbe goes into the house. Makhotin stands next to Anna who is looking into the distance towards Moscow.)

Makhotin: Why do you take such a hard tone with me? Haven't you any pity?

Anna: I have scorn. How dare you shake Vronsky's hand?

Makhotin: He shook the hand of Alexei Karenin.

Anna: Wretch!

Makhotin: And he's going to rejoin his princesses hell for leather. See who is worthy!

Anna: You lie—he is going to rejoin General Serpukhovskoy.

Makhotin: (laughing) The General! Ah, that's a good story!

Anna: (calling) Vladimir!

Makhotin: (still laughing) The General, the General!

Vladimir: (entering) Excellency.

Makhotin: Vladimir, the Barinia is calling you.

(Makhotin enters the house, still laughing.)

Anna: What shame! What shame! Vladimir.

Vladimir: Excellency.

Anna: Saddle a horse and get to Moscow as fast as you can. Go to the Nijni Station and get there before the train for Olsiralovka departs.

Vladimir: I will get there in time, Excellency.

Anna: You must get there in time. You will give this letter to Count Vronsky. If you can't find him, if he cannot come—return without delay to tell me. Knock on this window here. I will come. I don't want them to see you speaking to me.

Vladimir: As you wish, Excellency.

Anna: (writing the letter which she gives to Vladimir) "Alexei, come in the name of heaven! I'm afraid. It's a question of my life." (sealing the letter and handing it to Vladimir) Go, Vladimir and gallop, gallop all the way to Moscow.

(Vladimir leaves hastily.)

Anna: A quarter of an hour to go. A quarter of an hour to return. If Vronsky isn't here at eight o'clock—

(Voices call to Anna from inside the house.)

Barbe's Voice: Anna! Anna Arkadyevna!

Anna: I'm coming! I'm coming!

CURTAIN

EPILOGUE

Same décor. Black night. The open door of the house is brilliantly lit. No one is on the stage, then some children run onstage.

Nicolas: Softly. They can see you from the window.

Peter: No danger! They are eating! Come, do you have your trap?

Nicolas: Yes.

Peter: We'll surely catch a rabbit tonight. What luck, huh?

Nicolas: Hush! No! If the Barinia were to see us—

Peter: Chicken! Let's go. In five minutes, we will be back. Annoushka won't notice a thing.

Nicolas: Yes, let's go.

(The children disappear down the little stairway. A pause. Eight o'clock sounds in the distance. Vladimir appears at the top of the stair. He is covered with dust. He knocks on the window softly—then goes off to the right. A pause, then Anna's voice.)

Anna's Voice: No, no—just a little headache. I want to be alone in the air for five minutes.

(Anna comes to the door and calls.)

Anna: Vladimir.

Vladimir: Excellency!

(Vladimir gives Anna a letter.)

Anna: Then, the train had already left?

Vladimir: No, Excellency. You heard it pass.

Anna: That's true.

Vladimir: A slow machine, a half hour late at least. I got there before him.

(Makhotin appears in the door on the veranda. Anna doesn't see him. He puts his finger to his lips and listens unseen.

Anna: (reading the letter) "I cannot return before tomorrow at ten o'clock." (to Vladimir) And, did he say anything to you?

Vladimir: He said: "Here, my boy, take this to Anna Karenina." Then he went to rejoin the ladies.

Anna: The ladies?

Vladimir: Yes, the Countess Vronsky, his mother, then Princess Sarokine and her daughter. They all left for Obiralovka.

(Anna stifles a sob.)

Vladimir: Excellency?

Anna: What are you saying? Why do you tell me this? The Count was not alone?

Vladimir: No, Excellency. The Countess Vronsky, his mother, was with him and the Princess Sarokine and her daughter. I saw them choosing their compartment.

Anna: Be quiet!

Vladimir: Certainly, Excellency.

Anna: And go away. Go away, Vladimir.

Vladimir: Excellency—

Anna: Leave me. I order you.

(Vladimir goes.)

Anna: The wretch! The miserable liar! It's to these women that he went—the wretch—the coward.

Makhotin: (near her) He's an honest man, Anna.

Anna: You! You were listening! Spy!

Makhotin: There, there, pretty lady, no nasty words. I love you. Love excuses everything.

Anna: Love! Oh, you speak of your love.

Makhotin: Eh, yes. It's the only true one. The only sincere one. The loyal embrace, without phrases. Those who talk too much lie too often. Only the kiss alone exists for two young, beautiful, free beings.

Anna: Leave me!

Makhotin: Say yes! Tell me yes! You will see—

Anna: Leave me—coward—wretch!

Makhotin: And who would blame you? No one. The old girl there—she knows it—she encourages me.

Anna: What a shame.

Makhotin: And then, you are only my friend's mistress.

(Anna recoils to the stone balustrade and lets out a frightened cry.)

Anna: Ah, there—there on the railway track. There's someone. Help!

Makhotin: No one. There's no one.

Anna: Help! Oh, he doesn't hear me.

Makhotin: Oh, oh, useless. There's no one. We are alone.

Anna: Oh, he doesn't hear me. He cannot hear me. It's him! It's the little Mouzhik. The little Mouzhik! (suddenly, very low) Ah, it's he—who's calling me—he must iron it, mold it, crush it—

Makhotin: Come on, come on. I know this stuff. You want it. You want—it's the last comedy, right?

Anna: (her voice fixed) Yes, the last.

Makhotin: About time. Come then.

(Makhotin reaches out to take her. Anna pushes him away.)

Anna: (in a dead voice) Yes, yes. We will go in the park. Both of us. But, I'm cold, I'm very cold. Would you go find my cape?

Makhotin: I win! I adore you.

(Makhotin returns toward the house and disappears. Far, very far, the voice of the Moscow train.)

Anna: (alone) Here—nothing but mud. Down there—mud. Everywhere mud and shame.

(The voice of the train is heard in the distance.)

Anna: One must beat the iron. Yes, yes, you're right, old Mouzhik. (the noise grows) They are there, both of them, in the same compartment—the one beside the other—just like we were once. My little Seriozha! (the train arrives) Forgive me, Lord!

(Anna is at the little door and starts going down the steps.)

Anna: Vronsky! I am coming. I am coming, Vronsky. You will be free.

(Anna has disappeared. The growling of the train peaks, then passes like a gust of wind. There are plumes of black smoke, reddened by the fire of the locomotive. The smoke dissipates as the train passes and the noise lessens. We hear the children let out screams of fright and see them hurry towards the house which Makhotin is leaving, whistling, Anna's cape on his arm. He stops the two children.)

Makhotin: Well, what? Naughty little devils. What's wrong?

The Children: Anna Arkadyevna! Anna Arkadyevna—there—there! The train. Anna Arkadyevna!

Makhotin: What! What! What are you saying? Why are you crying like this?

(The children are terrorized. They point their fingers toward the train track.)

The Children: There! There! The train! Anna Arkadyevna!

(Makhotin pushes them brutally and hurls himself toward the track. The children are silent, frightened. In the distance, a long way off, the whistle of the locomotive is heard.)

Makhotin: Oh, help! Help! Help!

CURTAIN

MARLBOROUGH'S SONG
from Act I, Scene 1

Malbrough s'en va-t-en guerre,
Mironton, mironton, mirontaine,
Malbrough s'en va-t-en guerre,
Ne sait quand reviendra.

Il reviendra-z-à Pâques,
Mironton, mironton, mirontaine,
Il reviendra-z-à Pâques,
Ou à la Trinité.

La Trinité se passe,
Mironton, mironton, mirontaine,
La Trinité se passé,
Malbrough ne revient pas.

Madame à sa tour monte,
Mironton, mironton, mirontaine,
Madame à sa tour monte,
Si haut qu'elle peut monter.

Elle voit venir son page
Mironton, mironton, mirontaine,
Elle voit venir son page
Tout de noir habillé.

Beau page, mon beau page,
Mironton, mironton, mirontaine,
Beau page, mon beau page,
Quelles nouvelles apportez?

Aux nouvelles que j'apporte,
Mironton, mironton, mirontaine,
Aux nouvelles que j'apporte,
Vos beaux yeux vont pleurer!

Quittez vos habits roses,
Mironton, mironton, mirontaine,
Quittez vos habits roses,
Et vos satins brodés!

Monsieur Malbrough est mort,
Mironton, mironton, mirontaine,
Monsieur Malbrough est mort,
Est mort et enterré

Je l'ai vu porter en terre,
Mironton, mironton, mirontaine,
Je l'ai vu porter en terre,
Par quartre-z-officiers.

L'un portait sa cuirasse
Mironton, mironton, mirontaine,
L'un portait sa cuirasse
L'autre son bouclier.

L'autre portait son grand sabre,
Mironton, mironton, mirontaine,
L'autre portait son grand sabre,
Et l'autre ne portait rien.

On planta sur sa tombe

Mironton, mironton, mirontaine,
On planta sur sa tombe
Un beau rosier fleuri.

La cérémonie faite,
Mironton, mironton, mirontaine,
La cérémonie faite,
Chacun s'en fut coucher…

ABOUT FRANK J. MORLOCK

FRANK J. MORLOCK has written and translated many plays since retiring from the legal profession in 1992. His translations have also appeared on Project Gutenberg, the Alexandre Dumas Père web page, Literature in the Age of Napoléon, Infinite Artistries.com, and Munsey's (formerly Blackmask). In 2006 he received an award from the North American Jules Verne Society for his translations of Verne's plays. He lives and works in México.

www.ingramcontent.com/pod-product-compliance
Lightning Source LLC
LaVergne TN
LVHW041625070426
835507LV00008B/449